COFFEE
&
ORANGE BLOSSOMS

7 YEARS & 15 DAYS IN TYRE, LEBANON

NATE SCHOLZ

Phoenician
press

PHOENICIAN PRESS, LLC
STANWOOD, WA

Published by Phoenician Press, LLC
Stanwood, WA 98292
www.phoenicianpress.com

Nate Scholz, *Coffee & Orange Blosssoms, 7 Years & 15 Days in Tyre, Lebanon*
Copyright ©2013 by Nate Scholz

This book details real life events. Some names were changed to protect privacy. Events were condensed where it served to improve readability.

Cover artwork and photography by Nate Scholz
Cover and interior design by Timofey Lychik *www.lychikstudio.com*

For more information or to report errors, please contact Phoenician Press at *info@phoenicianpress.com*. Supplemental material, including maps and photography can be found at *www.coffeeandorangeblossoms.com*. Follow Nate Scholz's blog on complementary subjects at *www.N8exchange.com*.

First Edition

10 9 8 7 6 5 4 3 2 1

ISBN 978-0-9898711-0-5

For Naomi, Gideon, Elijah, and Zadek
… and the generations of their children
that follow while Jesus tarries.

Carry on…

CONTENTS

ACKNOWLEDGMENTS

My great grandfather, John Bertram, wrote The Story of Our Family in 1947. My wife Kimarie's aunt, Heather Johnson, recorded the story of her parents, Ted and Millie Ware, in With A Love. These family members demonstrated the value of passing down their own legacy stories to inspire Kimarie and me.

As I drafted this book, I imagined my great grandchildren as my primary audience. For their benefit, Naomi, Gideon, Elijah, and Zadek sacrificed some daddy time we could have spent together.

But my wife Kimarie labored the most by far in the birthing of this book. She edited my work in the evenings after the kids went to bed. The laughter and tears that accompanied her corrections encouraged me to delight her with my best efforts.

Lisa Ohlen Harris invested herself in this book beyond content and copy editing. She spoke of potential in my raw writing voice, and continued to proclaim it could be better until it was.

I owe a ton to my initial editorial team: Andrea, Anna, Dave, Denis, Edmond, Heather, Inger, James, Jeleta, Jenn, Jill, Jim, Jon, Ken, Kent, Kevin, Larry, Randy, Stan, and Steve. Those poor guinea pigs! They willingly subjected themselves to reading and marking up my first manuscript, Crumbs 1.0. Thankfully, that original draft of the book has little resemblance to what you now hold in your hands. If my first readers have the guts to open these pages, I know they'll experience the satisfaction of their contributions.

Thanks to Timofey Lychik for taking my never-ending requests for revisions on layout and cover design with professionalism and style.

Ken Smith went out of his way to attract the attention of noteworthy publishing houses. I was moved by his efforts.

Most importantly, I'd like to acknowledge my friend, Jesus. If I had never followed him, I wouldn't have lived this adventure.

PREFACE

The phone rang during our Tuesday morning family Bible time. A minute later, my mobile phone vibrated. "Someone must be serious about talking with you this morning," Kimarie said. I suddenly had a sense of foreboding, but we finished our devotions as planned. I extracted myself from the close cuddle with Naomi and Gideon and stepped around baby Elijah banging his rattle on the floor. I retreated upstairs to listen to my voicemail in the privacy of the bedroom.

It was Lisa, the consulting nurse at Mom's family care home. "Nate, I have some shocking news. Your mom died this morning – a few minutes ago."

I slumped on the bed and wept at the thought of her leaving without family at her bedside. It was February 10, 2009, and I was suddenly a forty-three-year-old orphan. *So soon?*

Mom had just spent Christmas with us in our home in Mount Vernon, Washington. She was fine then, bragging about her good health. Back at home on Vashon Island after the New Year, she had trouble breathing so a friend drove her to the emergency room. She was diagnosed with stage III non-small cell lung cancer. Suddenly, her days were numbered. Three to six months. Ninety to 180 days.

I thought about the last time I talked with her. I left her with *Practicing the Presence of God*, a classic book of faith by Brother Lawrence.

"Are you okay?"

"I'm fine." She smiled back.

"I'll see you on Wednesday, Mom. I love you."

"Drive safely. I love you too…"

Wednesday never came. She left us only six weeks after her diagnosis, her quick passing so unlike the lingering death Dad suffered.

I see clearly that we can't put off the things that are important for us to accomplish in life. Time offers no guarantees.

As the oldest son, I was assigned the role of executor of my parents' estate. My parents had a lot of stuff in their home. The family joke was, "If you go into the house and see two of something, it's the beginning of a collection." They spent their time in the not-so-nautical sport of garage sale-ing. Their pleasure in amassing artifacts became a burden to those of us left to deal with their impressive collections. My brothers and I conferred with each other and agreed that our parents' interest in this stuff had not transferred to us. It was up to me to figure out the most lucrative ways of liquidating their treasures, about which I knew very little.

The task I was charged with was depressing; to systematically rid the world of physical evidence that my parents ever existed. So often we are defined by the things we own. With my parents' things disposed of, the memory of their lives would disappear within the next generation.

I faced the question of my own purpose for living. It stirred an itching sense of responsibility to leave something behind. I want to be relevant in the lives of my children's grandchildren and beyond. I write to speak through time and deliver a legacy.

This is a book about being born again again. My first rebirth experience occurred in a mysterious moment of decision to serve Jesus: a singular, pivotal change of direction. It was a good start. From then on, small daily decisions to prioritize what I saw as God's plan continued to recreate me. Radical obedience made the difference between basic gratitude to a savior and living life with abundance and adventure.

I lived in the biblical city of Tyre for almost seven years. During that time I went through many normal stages of life, but those milestones gained the flavor of being lived out in the context of Shia Muslim culture. I want to share two stories here. The first is the day-to-day story of a flight from danger, laid out in the emails that I sent to family and friends during the July 2006 bombing of Lebanon in the thirty-three day war. The other is the story of seven years spent in the Hezbollah heartland of South Lebanon, from 1999 to 2006. Admittedly, much of what I'll share of this time period was from the first two years when I was new to the country and single and had the mental leisure to philosophize freely.

The email you are about to read represents the beginning of the end of my life in Lebanon.

From: Nate Scholz
Sent: Wednesday, July 12, 2006
Subject: Day 1 - Tyre, Lebanon

Just a quick email to reassure you all that we are okay, but definitely a little nervous and vigilant to our environment.

This morning, Hezbollah fighters kidnapped some Israeli soldiers in an effort to induce a trade for some Lebanese prisoners who have been held by Israel. The Israelis decided not to negotiate, but to launch a rescue effort. All four bridges over the Litani River have been bombed, probably to limit the ability to transport the kidnapped Israelis out of South Lebanon.

We know of at least one way we could still cross the shallow river by car, so we are not exactly trapped here. However, the current hostilities are fairly serious. They could either escalate or fizzle out quickly. We have no reason to believe that there will be any fighting in the city of Tyre itself, but we've limited our movement and raised our awareness of the situation in case we are required to leave suddenly.

Please pray that the conflict is resolved quickly, and for our safety and those of our friends here.

We will keep you posted as events become known to us.

Salaam,

Nate, with Kimarie, Naomi (age two), and Gideon (age one)

EXIT STAGE WEST

My first career was as a grocer on Vashon Island in Washington State. I filled shelves and rang up customers' orders. Occasionally, I bagged the stuff and carried it out to their cars. The job wasn't fulfilling. Between the ages of eighteen and thirty-three, I judged success by the volume of emptiness I created. Empty boxes...Empty conveyer belts... Empty carts... I spent much of my free time sitting on the beach, vacantly watching the waters of Puget Sound lapping against the seaweed covered rocks.

When I was twenty-two years old, I went to a play about the life of Jesus, which marked the definitive moment of change in my life. From then on my time outside of work was occupied with studying the Bible and with music. Two of my coworkers were brothers and musicians; Dan and Randy modernized old hymns and wanted to start a band. On impulse, I took out a $6,000 loan and bought all the sound equipment they needed to go on the road. I didn't know the first thing about running sound, but it didn't matter to me. I was determined to learn how. Even if I failed, it was more important to me that the band had what they needed to bless people with their music. I can't produce music, but I discovered that God gave me an ear for adjusting it. I picked it up easily.

It was fun while it lasted, but by the time I was twenty-five, Dan had gotten married and Randy was working a lot. The equipment was just sitting unused. Dan urged me to sell it and go to Bible school. I did some research and found that the cost to attend a local college was about the same as the value of all the sound equipment I had. I started looking for a buyer. Several months later I still hadn't found one. The fall deadline for registration was coming up. I was running out of time. In talking to the school's registrar, I discovered that their traveling music-ministry group was badly in need of new sound equipment. I tried to strike a deal to trade the equipment for a year's schooling, but it fell through in the final round of negotiations because of the tight cash flow of the college. I felt deeply that I was supposed to go study the Bible there. I was sure that's what God wanted me to do too. So, why wasn't it working out? In the midst of wrestling with my confusion, I went to a weekend music festival called *Jesus Northwest*.

I parked my old Ford Econoline van in a field with thousands of other overnight campers. In the morning, I saturated myself with the seminars held between concerts. After lunch, I retreated back through the bent grass to contemplate the teachings I'd learned and take a nap in my sweltering van. I drifted off amidst the teenagers playing Frisbee outside. When I woke up, I lay there drowsily for awhile and let my mind float over the problem of selling used sound equipment in a troubled economy.

A question suddenly rang in my mind, "Are you trusting the sound equipment to get you to Bible college, or are you trusting me?" I was stunned. I hesitated, and then mentally confessed, "Uh... the sound equipment." A pregnant pause followed and then, "Get rid of the equipment and see what I will do." God spoke the words as a patiently suggested command.

It was so clear and so right and so easy. It couldn't have been my own idea because I'm too selfish to think of something like that. The other thing that convinced me that I had just heard from God was the joy and excitement that tickled through me as I made my plan. The next day I would drive to the college with all the equipment and donate it to the school. I'd explain that I understood their financial limitations, but God had told me to give it to them anyway. If I were to be enrolled at the school that fall, God would see to it. If not, then I would do whatever else he wanted me to do.

The next day, I felt like Santa Claus as I unloaded the equipment and wheeled it into the reception area at the school. The front desk worker was dumbfounded. Clearly, this was not an everyday experience. Word traveled fast through the administrative offices nearby. Someone made a quick decision that they could waive my tuition for a year, but that I'd have to pay the room and board. I knew I still didn't have enough. I smiled and said, "If God wants me here, I'll be back." My friend Dan and my parents were moved to offer monthly financial gifts in the exact amount that I needed to supplement my weekend grocery store earnings. I moved into the dorm and started classes in September 1991. I was one of the oldest students enrolled at twenty-five, but I made friends easily with the younger crowd. I laughed with them at my habit of ordering steamed milk at Starbucks when we went out together. They all liked coffee and I was the one guy in the entire Seattle area who didn't.

In the first term of my studies, a special speaker came from Africa. He told stories of what God was doing to call Africans to follow Jesus. I had been to talks like this before and I was accustomed to being moved to tears at the news of God's work around the world, but something was different that day. The chairs were arranged in a horseshoe shape instead of in rows facing the front. I wasn't looking at the backs of heads in front of me. The angled configuration of the room allowed me to see how others in the audience were responding.

Nobody else wept.

I pondered this new discovery that I was impacted differently than others. I came to the conclusion that I needed to go and live in another country, see what God was doing there, and tell people what I knew about Jesus. The next question loomed. Where?

Over the next year I agonized over hearing hints from God about location. The places I didn't want to go came to mind first and I went through a process of elimination. I wasn't interested in living in Asia, or Africa, or South America at all. Australians and Europeans had already had the historical opportunity to know about Jesus. That left the Middle East and the Poles.

The land of Arabs and Jews had always been provocative to me. The classes I took fueled my fascination of Old Testament culture and history. I was also attracted by the allure of Mediterranean food, but it didn't seem appropriate to answer the question of where God wanted me to go founded on my food preferences as a picky eater.

A doubt crept into my mind that if I went to the Middle East instead of somewhere else, I would be missing God's will and just doing what I wanted to do. I decided to listen harder. God led me in a routine of mental gymnastics to sort out the confusion.

Let's say I go ahead and arrive at the place I want to go and spend my life there, loving Jesus and making him known. Then I die and go to heaven. God meets me at the gate and says, "Okay," in a sarcastic voice. "I guess I have to let you in, but I wish you would have followed my subtle hint back in 1989 that I wanted you to go to Antarctica." That didn't sound like God's style to me.

So what if I go someplace that I don't want to, in order to ensure that my own selfish desires aren't influencing me? Doesn't that assume that God's goal is to make me unhappy? That wasn't consistent with what I knew of him either.

Hmmm... Who gave me a love for Middle Eastern food, even though I can't stand other ethnic foods? How many people think it would be fun to move to the Middle East? Can I dare to think that these passions were God-given when I was created, so it would be my pleasure to live them out? I cautiously moved forward another step.

I decided on the Middle East, but still needed to narrow my search to a specific country. I heard of a Westerner living in Beirut, named Carl, and asked to receive his email updates. The first newsletter I got told of a trip to a village in southern Lebanon, where Carl was scheduled to speak under a circus tent full of Shia who had gathered to learn more about Jesus. My spine tingled as I read the story, and I thought, "I've got to go be a part of that." I set my long-term goal to go and learn from Carl in Lebanon.

I graduated with a degree in biblical studies in 1993. I decided to take a year off from the grocery store and travel with my school's music and drama ministry team. Six of us drove across the country in the team's van, towing a trailer full of musical instruments and sound equipment. I had come full circle and was now operating the sound equipment I had donated two years earlier. We performed music, acted out dramas and taught from the Bible. In the evenings we were hosted in the homes of audience members and answered questions about our plans for the future. I got used to saying, "I'm going to get debt-free and then go to Lebanon."

Three years later, I still owed on my sound equipment loan and college loans from a previous round of studies at a more expensive college. I had returned to my familiar job at the grocery store and fallen into comfortable patterns. One summer afternoon in 1996, I visited my friends Wilson and Gorette. We were sitting on stools around the counter in their sunlit kitchen, and I must have casually repeated something about my future plans in Lebanon. Wilson challenged me.

"You keep talking about paying off your debts and going to Lebanon, Nate, but then I see you spending money on baseball cards and going to concerts. If you really want to go, then you have to get serious about setting goals and working toward them."

"What do you mean?" I defended. In my mind, I had been moving toward my Lebanon plans as fast as I could by making minimum payments until the *someday* of financial freedom came along.

"Have you ever calculated how many years it will take to be clear of your loans at the rate you're paying them?" He asked. "And, aren't there other things you need to do to prepare aside from finances that you could get started on in the mean time? You should set a goal date to go and do whatever it takes to make it happen." I suddenly caught on.

I admitted he was right. I was thirty years old. Time was ticking away. I looked vacantly toward the ceiling as I imagined how life would change if I put a departure date on the calendar. It would be like installing a compass on a drifting boat and locking in a course.

Wilson helped me think through action steps. "What are you going to do for a living there? Won't it seem strange for you to look for a job in a grocery store when you don't even know the language? And how many Muslim friends do you have? What do you know about Islam aside from what you've read in books?"

All the shortcomings that Wilson talked about were added to my list of obstacles to overcome. I started by tripling my debt payments and enrolling in an Arabic language class in Seattle. I printed two years' worth of calendar pages and circled a goal departure date in 1999. Then I mapped all the tasks I needed to accomplish from week to week. Instead of lounging around watching videos on my days off, I had work to do. Wilson said some thoughtful words, God snapped his fingers, and I woke up from the comfortable sleep walking of wasted years.

Friends and family members noticed a change in my level of determination to go to Lebanon. I wasn't known to be courageous or prone to irrational behavior. I represented an unsolved mystery to them.

"How did God call you? Did you hear a voice?" My explanation did little to convince them. Wasn't it conceited of me to claim that I had been singled out by God for a special purpose? Didn't I know that it was dangerous in the Middle East?

They'd shrug and mutter, "Keep your head down."

Almost 2000 years before I was to set foot in the city of Tyre, the apostle Paul was challenged by well-wishers there. Disciples of Jesus in Tyre questioned the safety of his plans as he walked out the path that God directed.

> *We found a ship crossing over to Phoenicia, went on board and set sail. After sighting Cyprus and passing to the south of it, we sailed on to Syria. We landed at Tyre where our ship was to unload its cargo. Finding the disciples there, we stayed with them seven days. Through the spirit they urged Paul not to go on to Jerusalem. But when our time was up we continued on our way. All the disciples and their wives and children accompanied us out of the city, and there on the beach we knelt to pray. After saying goodbye to each other, we went aboard the ship, and they returned home. (Acts 21:2-6)*

What did it mean that Paul went on after being urged *in the spirit* not to go? Was he disobedient? Did he have an overriding sense that was also from the spirit? Paul's decision to ignore the prophetic advice of his fellow believers in Tyre brought him great suffering over the rest of his life and deprived him of his freedom.

Whether he was disobedient or not, God never abandoned him. Paul was brought before kings to give his defense and repeat the testimony of his calling. In a Roman prison, he was free enough to write letters to the believers in all the places across the world where he had traveled. He impacted the very capital of the Empire.

Did I dare place myself in the company of such a man? Could I introduce myself like he did in his letter to the Romans? "Nate. A servant of Christ Jesus, called to be an apostle, and set apart for the gospel of God." An apostle is simply *a sent out one*. It just means that I left my home to go somewhere new, to be with a different group of people than I normally would refer to as *us*. An apostle relocates to be with *them*.

I needed to connect with this place to which I felt sent. I hadn't made enough progress on my loan payments yet, but I went ahead and added a bit of debt to build some experience into my motivation. I applied for my first passport at age thirty-one, emailed Carl, and bought airline tickets for a preliminary visit in the spring of 1997.

From: Nate Scholz
Sent: Thursday, July 13, 2006
Subject: Day 2

Hello All,

Just checking in again to let you know that we are still alright.

As you have probably heard, the Beirut airport has been bombed by Israeli jets and is currently closed. We have no idea how much time it might take to repair and reopen. The port of Beirut is also being blockaded by Israeli gunboats. This leaves several land routes of dubious safety level into Syria as options for departing Lebanon. At the moment we have decided that the best course of action is to stay put, stock up on food, and lay low in our home, hoping for a resolution to the conflict.

It sounds pretty bleak, but for the time being we are still feeling reasonably safe. We are in a civilian populated city with few targets of interest for Israel associated with Hezbollah.

We have a large vehicle with four-wheel drive, which should be able to get us across the river in the event of full-scale invasion or something. In the past there have been clear indications of Israel's intent to enter. We are ready to wade the river if need be. There are many places in Beirut and farther north that would be quite a bit safer, that we are exploring as options for relocation.

We realize the dangerous possibility that we could become the "frog in the pot of boiling water" and we're attempting to guard against a mistaken perception of safety. The local reaction is mixed. Some of our neighbors are exceptionally nervous and others say they are used to it and aren't fazed.

We will continue to check in with information and word of our condition. I would like to say I will do this daily, but don't worry about us too much if I forget one day, okay? It is also conceivable that phone communications could be cut off, which would make it impossible to email as well.

Again, please pray diligently for everyone's safety here.

Salaam,

Nate

ENTER STAGE EAST

I felt super-charged with anticipation to actually be *going* after all these years of talking about it. Then, just a few days before the trip, I received a surprising email from Carl. His plans had changed. "I'm not inviting new people to work with me anymore." Shaken, I continued reading, "You should still come. I'll arrange for you to be picked up at the airport. You should visit some other friends of mine here in Beirut and in the South. Maybe some opportunities will come up." I would be in the country for ten days, making up my itinerary as I went along.

The Lufthansa jet descended over the darkness of the Mediterranean Sea. Only on the final turn before landing did the lighted hills of the city appear along the Lebanese coastline. Groggy, I eased myself down the stairs they had pushed against the side of the airplane and onto the tarmac. The humid weight of diesel exhaust suspended in the night air filled my lungs as if Lebanon was shaking my hand in introduction, "Glad to meet you." This quintessential smell was replaced by the aroma of stale cigarette smoke as I entered the airport. I hunted down my bag from among piles of luggage laid out on the concrete floor and emerged meekly onto the street. I was relieved that Carl's friend Samir had come to claim me.

I spent the short tour of Lebanon investigating four job possibilities. I was back to considering where God wanted me, and I wondered if I'd blown my chance of getting it right by stalling so long.

Carl told me that Denis was teaching English in the South. I visited him and his family for three days in Tyre. Denis's wife, Brenda, welcomed me into their home. Their daughters, Brianne and Emilie, were four and three years old. They lived on the sixth floor of a building facing the ruins of an ancient Roman chariot track. The hippodrome sits just to the north of the peninsula that connects the mainland to what once was an island, before Alexander the Great had his way.

The weather was hot enough to need fans, but the electricity to run them operated on a government schedule: six hours on, six hours off. The Israelis had bombed a power plant a couple months previously and the remaining infrastructure couldn't supply all the demand. On the second evening, we played a back-stabbing game of Risk, so perhaps my mind was pre-disposed to the violent imaginings that surfaced in my dreams that night. I went to sleep around 12:30 AM, trying not to think about cockroaches in the darkness.

Fifteen minutes later, I heard an explosion in the distance that sounded remotely like thunder, but too loud. Another five minutes, and I heard a stream of cars with horns blaring, driving into the city. In the delirium of half-sleep, I conjured up a picture of a building being bombed. I reasoned that the car horns were to clear traffic as injured people were being rushed to the hospital. After half an hour or so, it quieted down and I was left to fight the heat and my fear-induced nightmares. *Keep your head down, Nate.*

The next morning at breakfast, I anticipated a grisly report of whatever catastrophe had happened. Denis didn't know what I was talking about. I described what I had heard. I was sure that the whole of South Lebanon was falling apart. He just smiled and explained that there had been a wedding. What I had thought was a bomb had been a fireworks celebration at the outdoor reception. The honking cars were following the bride and groom in a parade through the city. It happened at the usual time for these things, around 1:00 AM.

Some people are the optimistic, glass-half-full type. The rest are pessimistic and think of the glass as half-empty. I represent a third classification of my own when I worry, "What if the glass breaks?"

Denis showed me around the city the following day. We prayed as we walked, for the people we passed. Nighttime fears dissipated. It felt to me like God was listening, pleased that we were taking the time to talk with him.

The modern city of Tyre is shaped like the head of a dog with its jaws open, roughly fifteen city blocks long and seven wide. We covered half the city that day, weaving in and out of alleys and main streets and avoiding the sidewalk for fear of falling debris from the buildings. Balconies overhead were war-damaged and had not yet been repaired. We greeted Denis's many friends on the way. His open, honest personality had won him a good reputation and popularity. My attention swung easily between enjoying the conversations that we encountered and the weight of history that we walked through.

Tyre was once famous. In Phoenician history, purple dye originated there. The merchants discovered and closely guarded the secret of extracting the color from murex seashells. The clothes they colored were more valuable, ounce for ounce, than gold. As Denis and I walked and prayed, I pictured Jesus wearing a purple robe, offering to clothe all the people around us in the royal color as heirs to his kingdom.

My last memory of that visit to Tyre was of Denis's family seeing me off in a taxi to head back north after a morning stroll through the centuries-old open air market. A generous produce salesman gave softball-sized lemons to the girls. They stood out amidst the background of dusty Middle Eastern commerce, wearing their matching pink frilly dresses. Each cradled their mammoth lemon in front of them with both hands. The surreal scene confirmed that we foreigners were out of place, yet denied it at the same time.

***

When I returned to the US after my quick trip to Lebanon, fellow believers gathered to hear about what I'd experienced. At the end of the first speaking event a flash of inspiration made me pause. An appeal came out of my mouth as quickly as the idea entered my head.

"I think I'm supposed to get help and guidance from some of you," I said. "If you want to be involved in a team of sending partners, working towards getting me to Lebanon, I hope you'll come and talk to me after the meeting." The twelve who responded included both close friends and strangers from different backgrounds. Together we formed what became known as the Seeders Team. At our first meeting, I asked them to help me expectantly ask God in prayer which of the four opportunities I should take from those I had investigated in Lebanon. I gave them each a printed handout, which listed advantages and disadvantages for each of the choices. Without sharing any of my own thoughts, I asked them to pray for the month between meetings and listen for God's answer.

I prayed and listened too, and became convinced that I was supposed to go to Tyre. But, by then I was kind of stuck. What if the other twelve people heard something different? How would I sort it out then? I couldn't just invite all these people to participate in holding me accountable to what they heard from God and then ignore what they had to say! *What if the glass breaks?*

The next meeting arrived. I didn't share my own thoughts first. I wanted to hear what they had to say. Everybody wrote down their answers and then I went around the room and asked each to share. One said she hadn't gotten a specific answer, but was convinced that God had already told me. The other eleven opened their folded papers one by one to reveal the simple word, "Tyre."

Glory! God gave the gracious gift of clarity for the next step.

***

I wanted to make Muslim friends. How would I do that from the pastoral seclusion of Vashon Island? I had to move away, but waffled. Moving to the city demanded a surprising amount of courage, a leaving-the-womb kind of courage. I'll confess that I didn't see how it would be possible. On Vashon, I was paying off my debts quickly by sharing cheap housing, paying $250 a month for rent, and making good money as a journeyman grocery checker. How was I ever going to keep on track with my financial goals? What were the odds of finding a good job and cheap housing instantly in Seattle?

How should I start? I doubtfully spent a day scouting options for housing and work around the multi-ethnic University District.

I heard of a program called the Language Institute for Refugees that was held in a church building. I thought it would be good to volunteer there and get some experience teaching English, so I made an appointment to talk with the director. She welcomed me as a trainee instructor. As an afterthought, on my way out the door I asked, "Oh, do you happen to know of any super-cheap housing opportunities near here?"

"No, I'm sorry. I don't." She answered, "But there's a bulletin board upstairs where people sometimes post rental vacancies. You might try that." I went up and scanned the printed index cards, tacked in neat rows. I spotted the one I was looking for: an opening in a shared house with five bedrooms, two blocks away, for $200 a month! I called the number, made an appointment for an interview, and went home. *Well, that was a productive day.*

A few days later, my boss found me stocking shelves down one of the aisles. "Hey Nate, I heard that your getting ready to leave the store and move to Seattle. We'll be sorry to see you go, but I know you've been working toward this for a long time. If you need a job over there I can put in a good word for you with my friend Steve, who manages a store in north Seattle." *Was this really happening?*

"That would be great! Thanks." I took the phone number he gave me and set up an appointment with the store manager.

The next time I went to Seattle, Steve led me through the swinging green doors, past the produce department, and up the creaky stairs to his office. The weekly newspaper ad was spread out across the table between us, awaiting his approval.

"Why are you moving to Seattle?" It was no time to be cagey, but I didn't know what the whole truth would do for my chances of getting the job. Deciding to be candid, I said, "I'm preparing to go to Lebanon to teach English and tell people what I know about Jesus." He blinked, "What are your expectations for working here at Ballard Market?" Encouraged by everything else that had happened, I faithfully charged ahead with a description of the optimal situation, completely disregarding how inappropriate my demands were. "I'd like to be hired at my current journeyman wage, but I don't want to work more than three shifts a week. I'll need Sundays off as well as Tuesday and Thursday mornings, so I can volunteer at the Language Institute. I don't know how long I'll still be here in Seattle, but my intention is to leave for Lebanon in a year."

He said a few words about how he admired my commitment to my ideals, and then asked, "When can you start working?"

In the same week, at the house interview, the existing housemates grilled me to make sure I wasn't a typical heathen college student. They didn't want wild drinking parties or drugs or girlfriend sleepovers. Some of the interrogators weren't completely convinced about me, but I was voted in by a slim majority and invited into the house.

My head spun. My last day of work on Vashon arrived and my coworkers threw a going away party. The banner on the wall read, "Thanks for sixteen great years!" I said goodbye to the known, the comfortable routine. The new person I became was born as I burned the bridge in my mind. *I won't be back.*

The following year continued to change me internally, but I wasn't alone. Everybody thought about change as 1998 became 1999, and we inched closer to the impending shift into a new century.

The challenges that Wilson presented to me instilled a hunger to improve my character for what was coming. I read a book on spiritual disciplines: prayer, fasting, giving, and Bible study among others. Which one should I start with? I wanted to take it easy on myself and choose one that I was already good at, but that wasn't the point at all. If I wanted to learn discipline, it would be by practicing the most difficult of them, whether I enjoyed it or not. Identifying fasting as the hardest thing on the list was easy. I had never willingly skipped a meal, and it didn't sound fun at all. But I was intrigued by what the book said about people who fast experiencing clarity of thought and a sense of intimacy with God. I expected that my physical hunger would transform to a spiritual one.

I chose Mondays, and resolved not to eat each week between Sunday night's dinner and Tuesday morning's breakfast. I figured it would also train me to respectfully participate in the Muslim Ramadan fast when the time came.

Another ingestion issue needed attention. I grudgingly accepted that a dislike for coffee was going to be a problem. I hated coffee. I manage to live thirty years of my life near Seattle, the coffee capital of the world, without finding a compelling reason to overcome my revulsion to it. I didn't have anything against caffeine, but I probably would have injected it before *drinking* that black, bitter stuff that had made my dad's breath smell so bad. In college, my preferred delivery package for caffeine had been Mountain Dew or JOLT cola. I couldn't even stand coffee-flavored candy.

Suddenly, my desire to be in Lebanon and interact well in its culture was more important to me than nursing my pet prejudice against a beverage. Coffee drinking is a cultural expectation there, not merely a preference from a list of available choices. One's honor requires compliance to social norms, and when they visit they drink stout, thick Arabic coffee. How was I to survive the dishonor of refusing to drink it when it was offered to me?

The alternative was even worse: to drink the coffee and have my face reflexively contort and grimace. The thought of the embarrassment I would cause both myself and my host would force a cold sweat to burst out all over my bald head. No, I needed to be able to drink coffee, and at least pretend convincingly that I liked it. I enlisted help from an artsy friend, Josey Peterson.

Josey always had one of her collection of vintage cameras ready, and the eye to catch an unusual angle from which to frame her subject. She brought out the best of people around her. She also loved coffee. We shared gallons of it in different restaurants that summer as I gradually acclimatized my tolerance levels.

We started at the restaurant with the reputation for the weakest coffee in town. I dowsed a cup of joe with multiple sugar packets and creamer until it looked more like pale hot chocolate. As I fought for control of my facial muscles, Josey would laugh and talk about wanting to go and photograph Lebanon while I was there. She was one of those rare people who crossed boundaries in my life. We met in college, and she became friends with my other friends from home. I vacationed with her and a bunch of others at the Shakespeare Festival in Oregon that August, just a month before my parents waved from my gate at SeaTac airport while I boarded my plane.

***

September, 1999. Two years had passed in a blur of activity. My debts were paid off, and the circled date on my calendar had arrived in a flash. I flew through the night with 165 pounds of earthly belongings nestled in the hold beneath my feet. *Living* in Lebanon was different than visiting. To keep me from indulging in homesick daydreaming, I concentrated on the expectation that I would grow old there. I pictured myself preparing for retirement in Lebanon to better empathize with the values of the other young men around me.

As I got off the plane in Lebanon, my attention snapped back to short-term survival. I had to navigate the airport routine of visa stamps, baggage claim, and customs on my own. Then I would find Denis for the two-hour car ride to Tyre before I could sleep.

A whole new airport had been built since my first visit. Instead of walking across the tarmac into a receiving area with discolored walls from a million cigarettes, I glided along a new jetway into a sparkling building. Where there once had been a cold concrete warehouse with luggage strewn around on the floor, a modern conveyer belt had taken its place. The change put me at ease until I discovered that one of my bags had not arrived. I stood in a long line at what looked like a service counter to find out what to do next. I was nervously aware how dependent I would be on the agent's ability in English. Denis was out there waiting. When I didn't come out right away would he wonder if I had missed changing planes in Germany? Would he wait or go home? *I hope this line moves fast.*

My experience with ferries and grocery stores had fixed in me a rigid respect for the power of standing in line. That respect and my fear of being left to spend the night in the airport disturbed me as I watched suit-clad men, and women in stiletto heels sauntering past the twelve of us who were already waiting not-so-patiently. They barged right up to the front and interrupted whatever the agent was doing with the one who had waited his turn. The most astounding thing was that the agent immediately helped the cutters first! Everybody acted as if nothing unusual was happening. I had a lot to learn. I wondered what it would be like to grow old in this place, but I had not yet taken my first baby steps in understanding. Thankfully, an hour later, Denis was still there to take me home.

I spent the first couple weeks at Denis's apartment. I didn't venture out for several days, but slept a lot from the fatigue of jet lag and a nasty stomachache. Denis could tell I was fearful of leaving the house without him to translate for me. He armed me with the word for "Hello," which is *Marhaba*, and mercilessly pushed me out of the nest.

"Marhaba... Marhaba... Marhaba..." I rehearsed as I descended the stairs and emerged abruptly into the active, populous city. I stood on the corner of the busiest intersection, about to cross, looking for an opening in the traffic that would allow me to survive the short jog. Go! Just as I arrived on the other corner, a middle-aged man came out of a nearby pharmacy. My path was going to bring me to within six or seven feet of him and the look on his face put me on guard. When he had caught sight of me, his eyes squinted and his brow furrowed. He turned his head to follow my movements with a steady stare as if to accuse, "You're an American! I hate Americans! I want to kill you!"

It was at this moment that my experience in grocery work proved its value in preparing me for Lebanon. I had been trained to follow the ten-tile rule, which states if you come within a distance of ten floor tiles from a customer, you pause to greet her. Reflex kicked in, but instead of "Hi, how are you today?" it came out, "Mahraba" – mispronounced, but with a smile. Instantly, the man's face transformed into a warm smile of his own, with his response, *"Ahlan wa sahlan,"* meaning "You're very welcome here." I kept walking past him, puzzled that he could change his first impression of hatred so quickly. Then it registered that it wasn't hatred I had seen on his face. The emotion he had expressed was intense curiosity, which looks the same as anger. If I hadn't been trained in business hospitality, I would have walked past that guy convinced that he was an enemy. Instead, I was encouraged to believe the best about people in my first impressions.

I had a few conversations over and over again as I met new people in Lebanon. It made me sound good in Arabic because I'd had plenty of practice with all the related vocabulary, and the series of questions played itself out predictably, almost like a script. I even began to anticipate the next few questions.

"You're from America?"

"Yes."

Then they would want to find out if I knew a relative of theirs who had moved to the States. Hoping to hear "Michigan" or "California" they'd ask, "What state are you from?"

I had reason to cringe at this question and be a little evasive. If I said simply, "Washington," then they would assume that I meant Washington, D.C., and add to the general suspicion that any American living in Tyre was probably a CIA agent. Instead, I took the longer road, though it usually ended in the same place.

"I'm from the city of Seattle."

"Yes, but which state?"

"It's just north of California."

"Which state? What's its name?"

"Washington State."

"Oh, the capital."

"No. The capital is a city by the same name, 'Washington, D.C.' on the East Coast. Washington State is a different place – on the West Coast. We have Microsoft, Boeing, and Starbucks."

This was often met with a dubious look as they told me about some relative living in Dearborn, Michigan.

"Have you met him?

"No, but America is a big place. It takes four hours to fly to Michigan from Seattle." That was too vast for them to accept as real. Often the follow up question came after a thoughtful pause and then a preamble:

"Life here in Lebanon is hard right now. We are suffering. There is no work, no opportunity. All the people here are looking for a way to fulfill their dream and escape Lebanon to go and live in America. You could teach English and make more money there. So why would you want to leave your family and come *here?* It's backward. It doesn't make sense. Can you explain it to me?"

I came up with lots of reasons, but none satisfied my Lebanese friends with any degree of completeness.

"There's no crime here. I can walk around at midnight and not be afraid of getting robbed."

"It's beautiful here. The most beautiful thing is the people, like you."

"Money and opportunity aren't everything in life. I believe God wanted me to come here to live and share life with you."

Despite all the evidence that moved me to come, after living in Tyre for only a few weeks, I faced an intellectual crisis. In America I had a pretty clear purpose for introducing people to Jesus. It was all about transformation. People were messed up through divorce, drugs, alcohol, adultery, theft, and so on. When people followed Jesus, they changed into new creations. They got better. They became good.

The friends I made in my new home were Shia Muslims. They didn't match this pattern at all. They already had a fear of the one, mighty and sovereign God of creation, and they had their own set of rules in Islam that they followed pretty strictly. They were already much better good people than the good people I knew from home. They didn't feel like they needed Jesus because they were good on their own without him. My understanding of the purpose for sharing my faith was challenged. The ideal that had brought me to Tyre was to help people for their sake. The answer to the question, "Why are you going?" from my friends in the States had seemed so clear.

"Why are you here?"

Though I didn't want to admit it to myself, the best answer I could have given at the time was, "I don't know why."

From: Nate Scholz
Sent: Friday, July 14, 2006
Subject: Day 3

A quick one for today.

We are still in Tyre. We spent the day listening to jets flying overhead on bombing sorties to various places around Lebanon and were glad that we didn't try to travel to Beirut.

This evening our neighbors thought that it was dangerous for us to stay the night in our house on the sea, for fear of Israeli gunboats possibly making reprisals for an attack on one of their ships. So, we are relocating for the night to Edmond's house. It isn't far away, but we are nervous about driving at night with our kids, for any distance.

We had a group meeting earlier today, and we all agreed that it is the safest option to stay here in Tyre. There haven't been any direct attacks on the city, but the road heading farther south from here has been hit on the outskirts of the city. If you have heard that Tyre has been hit, it's because the city of Tyre lies in what is known as the region of Tyre. Various parts of the greater region have been targeted.

Things do appear to be escalating and we continue to pray for some resolution.

Thanks so much for praying for us. We have been depending on prayers to keep calm and think clearly.

Salaam,

Nate

MILLENNIAL MONSTERS

Three months in Tyre was long enough to acquire a Tarzan-like language ability and a few Lebanese friends to practice it with. Denis hired Sadiq as our language helper, and we had already become brothers. He was the firstborn son of a taxi driver, struggling to help his dad provide for the family amidst a troubled economy. His disabled younger brother's health needs caused Sadiq to leave his studies in electrical engineering to work. Providence brought him to our language school, initially to install a ceiling fan. He was a tall, slender man with close cut black hair. A doctor had scared his mother by telling her that he would lose his sight before adulthood from a rare condition. At twenty-five years old, he still looked out through large brown eyes and a strong eyeglass prescription. Sadiq had no teacher's training other than being a willing native speaker, but was cautiously optimistic enough to befriend the foreigners and want to help us, and to learn from us. Sadiq was open to new and modern ideas, but also solidly grounded in his culture.

When the month of Ramadan started, Sadiq was fascinated to learn that I would observe the fast. "You'll fast just like us for thirty days? No food? No water from sunrise to sunset? Aren't you a *Christian?*"

I knew I faced a dilemma in responding to that word: *Christian*. In Lebanon, faith is not expressed as correct theological belief, but through conforming behavior. Being a Christian has more to do with eating pork, drinking alcohol, and wearing immodest clothing, than personally held beliefs about Jesus. If I said I was a Christian, I would imply that I engaged in all the assumed immoral behavior that he associated with that word. I didn't want to lodge an inaccurate picture of myself into his mind. But if I said, "No, I'm not a Christian," it wouldn't be true either.

"I'm a follower of Jesus," I said. "I don't believe the same way that you do about fasting, but I want to show my respect for your culture."

"So, what's the difference between a Christian and a follower of Jesus?"

"Good question."

Sadiq and I went over the subtleties I could explain in the language we had in common. He was learning English from me, and I was learning Arabic from him. The distinctions I made intrigued him. He watched me carefully to test my claims. The difference was meaningful enough to him to place me into the class of *Mu'minin*, "believers."

When he repeated what I'd said to his mother, I received a standing invitation to eat the evening *Iftar* meal to break the fast with them. She worried that I'd starve to death from not being able to cook adequately for myself. "When you eat food with us, you become part of the family," she told me. "While you're away from your real mother, I'll be your second mother."

***

For years I'd lived with a sense of subconscious dread, ticking down the years to this auspicious date of January 1, 2000, with wonder. *Isn't something important supposed to happen at times like these?* Anticipation was in the air, as if the universe were holding its breath in a pregnant pause.

I wasn't worried about the Day of Judgment, but technology threatened to end Western civilization.

Computers had been created since the last millennium and miraculously became indispensable to human life within the space of forty years or so. World finance, telecommunications, transportation, everything in the developed world was connected to computers, which had been originally programmed with a two-digit abbreviation of the year. No one knew what would happen when the internal clocks of these machines flipped to midnight on January 1, 2000. Potentially, the computers would think it was 1900, causing widespread system crashes from data corruption and timing inconsistencies. After discovering the risk, programmers feverishly developed software solutions to eliminate this *Y2K bug*. The major cities of the world planned their momentous New Millennium Eve celebrations while citizens stockpiled food and withdrew money from banks, just in case.

That year, Ramadan and New Year's Day overlapped, so I invited Sadiq to spend the last hours of the year with the Westerners at a Mexican fiesta. As the party started, we turned on CNN to watch for effects of the Y2K bug in New Zealand. The date was to change first there, since the International Date Line is in the Pacific Ocean. Nothing happened. *Whew!* Then again, did they have computers in New Zealand?

We waited until the sun fell below the horizon to eat dinner. On the Islamic religious TV channel, the long fuse on a cartoon cannon was lit by an invisible hand. The blast signaled an end to the day's fast.

I worried Sadiq wouldn't like the New Year's Eve menu. His normal diet was ground beef kabobs, eggs, homemade French fries, and Arabic bread, which he ate almost every day. His status as firstborn son meant his mother would fix him whatever he wanted. Despite my concern that Sadiq wouldn't like the food, I was curiously satisfied by the role reversal. Sadiq took his turn navigating the diplomacy of properly eating strange food in a new context. I watched his courageous first bites of Mexican food. He discovered he liked all of it: enchiladas, burritos, and empanadas. Another shared meal brought us closer together. We played card games and prayed together as we waited for time to pass.

The last few minutes melted before midnight, local time. Everyone in Tyre fixed their attention on their televisions, except the boys.

The boys were busy preparing for war.

An arms cache had been stockpiled. Thousands of cheap Roman candles emerged on the street, pointed, and fired in all directions. An air assault rained down from balconies on combatants below.

New Year's Eve was the occasion for fireworks in Lebanon, not Lebanese Independence Day. Unlike the Fourth of July in the United States, Lebanon's independence from France was mostly ignored. There wasn't much to celebrate. They were still occupied by Israel and Syria. Real independence continued to elude them.

I was glad for the safety of my observation post. Boyhood pyromania unleashed was nothing to be trifled with. Even more impressive were the tracer shells glowing red in streaks across the night sky from the anti-aircraft batteries in the hills, firing rounds into the sea: celebratory gunfire like the Wild West.

We surfed channels between the coverage of the party going on in Beirut and footage of the worldwide event unfolding. In each time zone we witnessed evidence of reckless abandonment in the revelry. People were desperate to bring meaning to this moment, to be able to look back and recall some wild experience on a singularly memorable night.

We watched the world's great pyrotechnic displays. My favorite was in Paris, with the Eifel Tower as the backdrop. The next hour showcased the Millennium Wheel in London. At 3:00 AM I was grateful for the break the sparse population of the Atlantic Ocean granted me to go home for a few hours of sleep.

I didn't bother getting up to watch Seattle's footage in the morning. US Customs officials had caught a terrorist at the Canadian border a month earlier, uncovering a plot to set off explosives on New Year's Eve at the Space Needle. The city called off the annual celebration at the Seattle Center and the police chief warned on the news of arrests if people showed up.

Midmorning, I awoke on the first day of the next thousand years and decided to go on a field trip with Sadiq. "We have to do something different today," he said. "No Arabic study. It's a holiday."

We were on our way to the town of Qana, about ten minutes' drive from Tyre in the hills to the southeast. I was in the passenger seat, and Sadiq sat in the back of a borrowed four-door sedan. We hadn't gone too far on the winding roads before we noticed that the friend who drove us had been drinking the night before and was still under the influence. His steering and speech were proof, despite his denials. I risked offending him by fastening my seatbelt. Seatbelts, in Lebanon, are normally only used for decoration, like parsley on a plate of hummus.

Thankfully, our trip was just 7 miles long. Our driver rolled down his window to ask directions, then carried on, weaving up through a labyrinth of narrow roads. Three-story buildings shaded the streets, planted on their edges with no sidewalk. Customers had to look both ways before stepping out of a shop.

Our driver turned left at a nondescript driveway and into a barren hillside parking lot. We were at our destination, but I was still fuzzy on what we were there to see.

"The ruins are famous," Sadiq said, as we got out of the car.

We walked across the parking lot toward a trailhead guarded by a seventeen-year-old Lebanese soldier, cradling an automatic rifle in the crook of his arm. We cautiously approached, but he smiled, greeted us, and waved us on. We were left to wonder if he was keeping the archeological site safe or if the hill was somehow militarily strategic at the moment. Sadiq and I walked past the camouflaged tank and wandered along a vague trail between outcroppings of jutting limestone, laid bare by ancient winds. Just then the air was still enough to allow the lazy glide of a small white butterfly as it crossed our path.

We descended the sloping edge of a river canyon and could see for miles all around. The lone building far below was a stone structure, probably used by shepherds. In the massive rocks along the snaking path, we noticed acid-rain-washed carvings, pocked with holes from exposure to the elements. One cottage-sized stone had twelve human figures lined up in a row, chiseled there in antiquity.

I still didn't understand everything because of our language gap: his English, my Arabic. We negotiated meaning, committing ourselves to the hard work for the sake of our friendship.

"These are the twelve friends," Sadiq had said.

"Whose friends?" I asked.

"Jesus' friends," he said, exasperated at my inability to grasp the obvious. The usual translation for *disciples*, it turns out, comes across as *friends* in Arabic.

We walked on for another ten minutes or so. At the end of the path was the "Grotto," a cave tall enough to walk into and comfortably accommodate six or seven people. The darkened walls and ceiling bore witness to countless campfires. Light shone in through a large crack from above, just above a natural ledge. The cave's only decoration rested there: an eight by ten inch paper icon of the "bleeding heart" Jesus. Wax drippings hung in layers along the shelf, hinting at the legacy of midnight vigils held in both the distant and more recent past. Two candles stood, still lit, next to the picture.

Sadiq made the final push to communicate the relevance of the place to me. "This is where Jesus did his first miracle." Miracle was a new word. "He turned water to wine." Wine was a new word.

"Oh!" I said, as the similarity between Qana and Cana finally clicked in my head, "The wedding feast?" It didn't look like a great place to hold a wedding to me. "Isn't Cana in Israel?" I skeptically suggested.

"No. That's a big lie," Sadiq argued. "The crusaders made that up. There aren't any ruins there."

I wished I understood him better and resolved to work harder on my Arabic. Later, I learned that the remains we saw were from an early monastic order. The brotherhood chose to live in the cave in this holy village. The Lebanese claim Qana is the true site of the wedding feast. The monks commemorated Jesus' local miracle with their engravings.

Whether or not Jesus had actually been there, Sadiq – my Muslim friend – had gone out of his way to share a faith connection. He had something else to show me nearby and we parked again, just a few blocks away. Qana was famous for other reasons. Not all of the village's history was ancient.

In the spring of 1996, a three-year-old ceasefire agreement between Hezbollah and Israeli forces collapsed, and fighting began again in earnest. Each side escalated retaliation for atrocities. They pointed their fingers at each other to excuse their own blame with the well-worn adolescent words, "They started it!" This brief sixteen-day clash was known as "Operation Grapes of Wrath." By April 18, the Israeli military had warned civilians to flee their homes in the line of fire, but most of Qana's inhabitants were too poor or had no transportation options and nowhere else to go. Eight hundred chose to shelter in the UNIFIL relief tent at the UN headquarters nearby. That day, Israel targeted the peacekeeping base and fired thirty-eight 155 mm anti-personnel shells. One hundred and six civilians died.

Most of the casualties were women and children.

Three years later, as Sadiq and I approached the place where it happened, the memorial building was still in the early stages of construction. A plot of ground had been designated for mass burial. Rows of marble tombs stretched out across a yard encircled by a wall of photos, showing the last living depictions of the victims captured on film.

A caretaker made his way over to us as we respectfully explored. He surprised me with his English skills as he explained what I'd noticed. A common last name was engraved on many of the tombs.

"This section is for the family of Saadallah Ali Belhas. He and his son were not here. They survived. But thirty-one of their family members were killed in the massacre. Each of the two men lost his wife. Twelve of their own children were taken from them."

I didn't know what to say. What could I say? Instead of talking, I paid my respects, standing in solemn silence before the school portraits of the dead children.

Our guide pointed toward a building up some stairs I had initially overlooked. "There are more photos up there," he said. It was his job to tell the story faithfully. This was his home. For him the memory was always fresh.

We softly stepped up to the temporary wooden structure and were confronted with more graphic photos of the massacre. I didn't want to be there, but I forced myself to continue looking at sights that no one should ever see. I was stricken by a particular photo of a relief worker holding up the top half of an infant by the arms for the camera – the baby's entrails hung down below. I swallowed hard and felt sick.

Sadiq stood quietly next to me. His face contorted as the scenes refreshed his own memory. I learned the story as our guide translated Sadiq's words. "I was here. I was a volunteer with the Lebanese Red Cross when this happened," he said. "The world must remember what Israel did. This should never happen again."

He was an eyewitness to the aftermath. It could've just as well been him in that photo, holding the child. I couldn't talk for grieving. Involuntarily, my imagination placed me back in time with Sadiq. *What would I have done if I'd been there? How would it have changed my life?*

Somber, exhausted, we returned to the car and drove home to Tyre. I needed time alone to reconstruct my blasted mind. It was too much: *water to wine, grapes of wrath, the first day of the next thousand years.* My new friends in South Lebanon had greater terrors to fear than a measly Y2K Bug.

After I wrote that message last night, we reconsidered braving the roads and decided instead to move the children into our room with us for the night. Their room has only a window and a wall between it and the sea, while our room has five walls. We didn't sleep well because we continued to hear jets and bombs throughout the night. Most of the sounds were in the distance, but half a dozen or so sounded quite a bit closer to the city.

This isn't all that fun. Our nerves are a bit frayed, and I am starting to notice that my blood pressure feels elevated. The children are hanging in there, but are also being affected by the tension in the air. We adults are trying to remain visibly calm for their sakes.

This morning we are reconfirming that we are registered with the US Embassy in Beirut. They haven't contacted us in any way, so we think that maybe they don't remember we are here.

We still have no reason to believe that Israel will start hitting civilian targets that don't have anything to do with Hezbollah. So it continues to seem wise that we sit still and ride it out rather than put ourselves in harm's way on the roads.

Somehow, ironically, the government electricity has remained on for a longer percentage of the day than it was before the conflict started! I would have expected that we would be without power from the beginning. People in the city are mostly indoors, but there are some who have continued taking strolls on the sidewalk, and we can still hear children playing outside.

I thought it might be a good idea to let you know who we are consulting with. Our group consists of the three families who are connected to the language center I work at. The Scholz family includes me and Kimarie and our kids Naomi and Gideon. My boss Denis's family includes his wife Brenda and their kids Brianne, Emilie, and William. Edmond is the owner of the language center. He is with his wife, Roberta, and their son Jad. We've decided to stick together through this and make our decisions by consensus.

Well, I'll try to check in again later in the day to fill you in on anything new. Please continue to pray. We are feeling God's grace as he responds to your cries on our behalf.

Salaam,

Nate

DRIVE

The horn honking, light flashing, double-passing system of Lebanese traffic was as foreign and scary as the language. The stoplights and stop signs familiar to me back home in the US were replaced by large swirling traffic circles. Everyone drove fast enough and close enough together to make side-view mirrors an endangered species. Divided freeways were new to Lebanon and there were only two of them, running the length and width of the country.

Day or night, flashing your lights said, "Watch out for me," to oncoming traffic that might be straying too far over with no painted lines to guide them. Honking the horn signaled to the driver in front that you were about to zoom past them on the left, whether there was room to pass or not. It took dexterity to work the lights and horn simultaneously when passing one vehicle while warning oncoming traffic to veer out of the way. Pedestrians on the side of the road sometimes had to sidestep to avoid being hit.

Street lamps were few, and seldom was there electricity to light them at night. Drivers had to memorize the location of the potholes.

Evening social visits brought families, dressed in Shia black, out to stroll along the sides of the roads. Pedestrians turned invisible to drivers squinting into the glare of oncoming headlights, left on the high beam setting by default. Add rain to the mix and it was the perfect recipe for white-knuckles on steering wheels.

After arriving in Lebanon, I decided I didn't have the nerve to drive and resolved to hitch rides with friends or use the many options for public transportation. The first time I drove it was because it would have taken greater courage *not* to drive myself.

Sadiq suggested we use part of a four-day holiday weekend in January to tour around Lebanon's coast north of Beirut. Maybe it was the prophet Mohammed's birthday. I hadn't left Tyre in several months except to shop for furniture, so I was excited to explore. I broke out my copy of the Lonely Planet travel guide for Lebanon and extensively planned a route of sights to see on our trip. I especially wanted to wander through the Crusader castle in Tripoli.

We left on a Sunday afternoon, rented a Hyundai, and picked up Sadiq's friend Walid. I assumed that the other two would do the driving, but quickly found out I was by far the more experienced driver. Walid didn't drive at all, which was funny because he would later become my auto insurance agent. Sadiq could drive, but had exaggerated his abilities. I was surprised when he handed me the keys for a first turn at the wheel. I ventured out nervously, expecting the worst. When I was personally in control of the vehicle, I didn't find traffic nearly as scary as when I was reacting to the chaos as a passenger.

It took us three hours in heavy traffic to get to Beirut, and I got my first taste of bumper-to-bumper and door handle to door handle driving. I concentrated on proximity awareness and somehow managed to survive the journey without a scratch. The other drivers were just as anxious as I was to avoid collisions. I sweated the process of parallel parking on a narrow street below Walid's college apartment, where we spent the night.

The next morning, Sadiq took the first turn driving, and I was glad it wasn't up to me to navigate the maze of Beirut during rush hour traffic.

Our first stop was to check out the snow on Mt. Lebanon. We turned right at the coastal city of Jounieh and slowly made our way up the mountain road switchbacks to the ski resort town of Faraya. The base of the ski area had no lodges, so we brushed the snow off some plastic chairs and sat and drank hot chocolate outside one of the snack shacks. It was weird to think of my factory-working friends back home on Vashon Island having made the K2 skis I saw people carrying over their shoulder on the way to the ski lift.

We took a little hike up a sledding hill through snow up to our thighs. Sadiq and Walid had never experienced snow. They were playing like little kids, throwing snowballs with their bare hands. None of us had dressed warmly enough, but Walid was the worst off. His black dress shoes weren't helping to keep his feet warm. After twenty minutes, we were too cold to continue. They thought I was superhuman when I safely drove us back down the mountain on freshly snow-covered roads.

By the time we got to the Crusader castle it was mid-afternoon and sprinkling rain. To Seattleites, rain means nothing. If we let rain stop us from going outside, we'd never leave our homes. Rain means something to Lebanese. Sadiq slowed down as we drove by the gate. "It looks closed to me," he said. A fleeting glance of the drawbridge gate was all I got.

Instead, we went to visit a high school friend of Sadiq and Walid's in the Maronite Christian border town of Zghorta. We were there for hours and were invited to eat lunch with the family. I caused a scandal by refusing their hospitality. I had continued to fast on Mondays since before moving to Lebanon. The trip to the north and this visit with a family just happened to overlap awkwardly with my weekly practice.

We were served cake on small plates and glasses of cola in the living room. After awhile, it was noticed that I wasn't eating the cake. The hostess wondered, "Would you like something else?" She was pleasant, but I was clearly expected to receive their hospitality graciously.

"Oh, no thank you. I'm not eating today," I said. I hoped to get the opportunity to begin a discussion on faith. Sadiq tried to smooth over their confusion, but he was embarrassed.

"He's fasting."

The Catholic family members in Zghorta were perplexed. I didn't make sense to them because I wasn't fasting like a Muslim. I wasn't following the daylight rules of fasting from sunrise to sunset, and I was only fasting from food; I *did* drink the Pepsi!

Neither was I fasting like Lebanese Christians, who don't stop eating, but just change the menu to fish. My timing was also off. Ramadan had already ended and Lent had not yet started. I could almost hear them thinking, *What kind of crazy religious nut is this who follows a fast of his own invention as if God would make up a special religion just for him?* They made a game out of tempting me by continually offering food to test my resolve.

Eventually, the topic of conversation shifted and I had managed to avoid being held down and force-fed. I was uncomfortable staying so long with this family and felt like we were wasting time that we could have been using seeing historical sites. I wanted to make the time memorable by what we did together. It was the flip side of Sadiq and Walid's motivation. They wanted to make the time memorable by spending it with people. The noteworthy place, the famous historical site, meant nothing to them. It was about the obligation to pay the visit, to share a meal.

I found myself disappointed in the trip because we had spent all that time driving and only minutes at the places I had looked up in the Lonely Planet guide. To my mind, we'd wasted the time sitting in a living room making small talk. I had overlooked a core value of society. It would have been better that day if I would have given up my own pride of a fasting discipline and preferred the new discipline of receiving hospitality graciously. So what if I'd had the opportunity to speak about my faith? I'd drawn attention to myself, but managed to avoid reflecting Jesus.

I drove the whole way home after nightfall. The streets were calmer, but bright lights glared in my eyes from the headlights of oncoming traffic. I felt liberated and wanted a regular dose of the power of self-determination that came with a car. I missed the freedom of driving. I knew I wouldn't continue to be satisfied to the limitations of the hours and routes that taxis normally operated. To a passenger, the traffic patterns *appeared* lawless. Lebanon's roads were a ballroom floor, and driving on them was like learning a new way to waltz. Following the rhythm, I found it oddly elegant.

Now that I had overcome my fear of the traffic dance, I was in the market for a car. The daily humiliation of language learning had left my bruised ego the challenge of proving that I was a capable adult. I needed a pressure-release valve to express some control over my surroundings.

***

March was when the weather suddenly got much warmer and orange blossoms released the most intoxicating perfume. The scent floated on swirling breezes. A momentary shift in the wind would saturate me with a cloud.

I patrolled my surroundings for cars, and took note of available makes and models. Vehicles maintained their value well on the secondary market because of high unemployment and the abundance of auto mechanics who wanted to attract regular customers with low labor fees so they could feed their families. There were two ways to go about buying a car in Lebanon.

Expensive cars that were less than ten years old could be found at the used car lots scattered around town. BMWs and Mercedes were common because the best, nearest place to ship cars from was Germany. The government of Lebanon prohibited the import of cars older than ten years, so if you wanted a cheaper, older car as I did, you had to use another method, which I found hilarious

"Look out for a car that you like," Sadiq said. We drove along the main drag of Abou Deeb Street. It was cruising time at dusk and families had piled into their cars. The seven-block stretch of road was clogged this time every day. Drivers followed the next vehicle's bumper a foot at a time between the two traffic circles at each end of this artery of the city.

I spotted a small, red, Honda CRX, moving toward us in the opposite lane. I'd seen it before. Small, sporty hatchbacks were rare in Lebanon, so the few were noticeable. I pointed, "There! What about that one?" Sadiq's friend, who was driving, rolled his window down and stepped on the brake. He gestured for the other driver to wait by holding up his hand with the fingers and thumb facing upward together. We both stopped, along with the entire city's evening traffic behind us.

Sadiq asked, "Is your car for sale? How much do you want for it?"

"I don't want to sell it, but I'd take four thousand dollars." The other guy had four friends with him, scoping out the teenaged clusters of girls gossiping their way along the sidewalk.

I was amazed that this shopping method was okay. So much emphasis was normally put on avoiding the "Evil Eye." Belongings were cursed if anyone gave them an envious glance. I thought that asking someone if their vehicle was for sale would be like hexing them to their face.

"That's too much!"

A horn honked behind us.

"How about three thousand, two hundred?" Sadiq countered.

Two short beeps from behind them.

"No, really. I can't." He said it with an inviting expression, looking for a higher bid.

"No problem." said Sadiq, "Let us know if you change your mind." We drove on and the search continued. "See Nate, those little cars are too expensive. You need a normal car that's bigger, like an older Mercedes."

I wasn't being agreeable about the kind of vehicle that they thought I should want. The last car I had owned was a sub-compact Subaru Justy hatchback, which I loved because it zipped around in traffic and was easily parked. I could see how those features would also benefit me in Lebanon. But my thoughts about a small hatchback were met with frowns. For some reason, all the cars people kept showing me were larger four-door sedans. Once again I was in conflict with a society where the community governs individual decisions.

I was further schooled in counter-intuitive laws of economics. Lebanese were fearful that small cars were unsafe. They didn't have many accidents, but the ones they had were monumentally bad. There were either minor fender-benders or high-speed fatal wrecks. People wanted stronger, heavier cars. Since small cars were unpopular, and they were more expensive, not as many dealers had them. Replacement parts were scarce. Fewer mechanics knew how to work on them. They were harder to sell when you wanted to get rid of them. After a great deal of frustration from both my friends and me, a compromise was reached. We agreed to find a two-door Honda Accord hatchback.

Mustafa was the hero who tracked down a clean, mechanically sound car parked on a side street in the city. I test drove it and the only thing it lacked was air-conditioning, which Mustafa assured me I could add later. He helped me start the buying process and used up a second day that he should have spent working in his shop.

Mustafa was the classic entrepreneur, always looking for the buy-low, sell-high opportunity. He had researched the used air conditioner market in China and found that shipping containers full of lightly damaged, split-unit home air conditioners were available. He developed a business with his brothers in buying these container loads and refurbishing them to sell to overheated homeowners in South Lebanon. His shop was just around the corner from my apartment.

Mustafa wore expensive clothes and talked fast. He had gained access to the more elite circles of businessmen in the city who met together in the evenings at the Tyros restaurant – the movers and shakers of local finance and prestige. For some reason, he adopted me as a friend, and was using his clout to fix me up.

I fearfully climbed onto the moped behind Mustafa and we raced off to the bank, swerving in and out of the slower vehicles on the road. I had to pay in cash. Checks and credit cards weren't used in Tyre. He used his cell phone to call the local official in charge of car paperwork, who came and met us in a parking lot. He took the previous owner's daftar, which was the small, plastic registration card, and began the process of transferring the title into my name. We scooted back to the former owner, got his signature and paid him.

After all the help Mustafa gave me, he insisted that I drive to an auto shop where he paid $20 to have the muffler replaced. My aim had been to assert control over an aspect of my life, and yet in the process I was humbled once again by the hospitality that was inflicted upon me.

I didn't know then how timely it would be to have a car during orange-blossom season of that particular year. Just two months later, I would be given an historic opportunity to drive some of my friends to their liberation.

Dear Family and Friends,

We went out for a fifteen-minute walk around our neighborhood this afternoon to try and find diapers. It felt so good to get out and breathe a little fresh air and stretch our legs after being cooped up in the house for four days. Not many people were out on the street, though, so we'll continue to stay home as we have been doing.

Tyre experienced more shelling in the area today. Gas stations all around the country were targeted. Two carloads of people trying to flee to a safer place were hit. Ten to twenty died in the blasts, including women and children.

Considering this, we are still going to stay put in Tyre. However, if there is a clear lull or cease-fire in the attacks, we have decided to drive to an area north of Beirut that is closer to our embassy. This will put us in a better position to be evacuated if that becomes possible.

We re-registered with the Embassy in Beirut today to make sure they know we are here. They still haven't acknowledged receiving our emails. We understand that they are trying to arrange for emergency transportation for American citizens to Cyprus. However, we anticipate that we would first need to make our way to Beirut. We aren't willing to attempt the move unless we are sure there will be a break for safe travel on the roads.

At this point we are assuming that the embassy is contacting people who have registered with them, to update them on advice or at least to confirm that they know where they are. Since we haven't received a confirmation, we believe that our registration has not been received and that we are on our own.

I apologize for those of you who want answers to questions in emails. I'm afraid that these mass email reports are all I have the energy to write right now.

Your prayers, petitions, and tears are warmly received, and we hope that God is being your comforter in this difficult time as well. Perfect love casts out fear.

Your witness (for Christ) on the scene,

Salaam,

Nate

SWEET SOLITUDE

"Come! Sit and have tea!"

"In a little while," I said. "I have to go exercise first." Mustafa's disappointed look told me he didn't want to accept my postponement. I persisted. "I'll drop in on my way back."

The friends I made were strewn in their shops all around my rented apartment, impossible to avoid as I ventured out on foot to work off the extra calories collected on my gut from previous visits. Learning Arabic merely required drinking a thousand magic glasses of heavily sugared tea. Mustafa released me with a nod at my promise and I improved my stealth mode, slipping undetected by the jeweler and the tailor's shop at the end of the block.

Now back to that woman Jesus called a dog.

I hated running. If not for a recent discovery, I would have continued with the more preferable morning habit of whacking the evil snooze button on my alarm clock. Twenty-seven minutes. Nine minutes times three repetitions.

Reading the Bible *before* running made the tedious rhythm of exertion tolerable. I discovered that Tyre is mentioned sixty times in the Bible. I wondered what it was about this historically pagan place that would have attracted God's attention enough to make it the third most mentioned city in the scriptures? *That* was a mystery that could get me out of bed in the morning to ponder.

I'd get the coffee going, sit at my little kitchen table and load up by reading one of these passages several times before going out to run. Exercise woke up my brain to mentally wrestle with what I'd read. Deep thinking engaged my mind enough to overlook the discomfort of running. Thoughts organized themselves into streams of dialog that felt like prayer. The verses I'd read that day in Matthew chapter fifteen were about a Phoenician woman – probably a worshipper of Melkert, a god associated with pagan Baal and Astarte. She had tracked down Jesus, who was somewhere on the outskirts of Tyre. He was trying to find some place he could escape the crowds. I visualized the scene playing out.

Jesus was quiet as this pagan woman pleaded with him for healing. Her daughter was possessed by a demon.

"Have mercy, Son of David!"

Jesus' followers, surrounding him, said to send her away.

She tried again, "Lord, help me!"

Then Jesus said something unexpected. "I was sent only to the lost sheep of Israel."

My friend with the water purifying business interrupted my thoughts from across the street with a greeting. I responded in Arabic then turned and waved into the open door of the computer shop I was passing. I wasn't completely free to lose myself in thought yet, still navigating my path to the ruins. The route was a straight road of six blocks, teeming with city life and traffic. I kept alert, not wanting to miss a chance at learning something new of my adopted culture. The green of the undergrowth beyond the fence came into view as I strode forward.

Almost there. Solitude.

"It's not right to toss the children's bread to their dogs," said Jesus.

The woman didn't let up. She threw herself to her knees. "Yes, but even dogs get crumbs off the table." Something about the moment changed his attitude. Jesus told her how much faith he saw in her, and her daughter was immediately healed.

I turned right, along the wide sidewalk where the road bent.

I followed the chain link fence and sidestepped a sticky patch of yesterday's melted ice cream. Head lowered, I dropped my shoulder in a well-practiced maneuver through a narrow gap in the fence without touching a link. Just a few feet beyond, it already felt quieter. Lines of ants criss-crossed the dirt path. I crouched to watch a team of them working to heft a dead cockroach and begin the journey to someplace miles away. I picked up three rocks and spun two between the fingers of my left hand, the other ready in my right – just in case the wild dogs were lurking around again...

The trail crested in a clearing, then ambled down and to the left among the yellow-flowered Scotch broom. Before the final descent of the trail, I stood a moment to survey the land of the hippodrome. No one else was there. I had the place all to myself.

In ancient Tyre, the Roman chariot track provided entertainment. Only a few lengths of grandstand remained, restored by archeologists. Once, the two-thirds mile track had been ringed by seating for 40,000 spectators. I entered the track through an arched limestone doorway, which had served as the southern entrance. Good timing. An hour or so separated the regular exercise time of Tyrian locals and the arrival of paying tourists in buses from Beirut at the far entrance on the north side. The discreet hole in the fence was tolerated by the guards, and left for the use of neighbors who came early and were clearly there to work out.

It was already hot for March, to my mind. The air was heavy with humidity and the sweet perfume of orange blossoms. Pushing against a fallen stone pillar to stretch my calves, I prayed, "Lord Jesus, what do you want me to know about you from your response to the Phoenician woman?" Why was this obscure event surrounding a Gentile woman recorded in the Bible as more important than any of the untold stories from his ministry?

I listened and began to jog counter clock-wise around the track with the sun in my eyes. I smiled at the irony of choosing this place to worship God as I passed a small altar to Melkert in the center of the track. My thoughts returned to Jesus.

"Jesus withdrew to the region of Tyre." I commiserated with his wanting to get away for some time to rest and think. He was tired, just like I would have been. Jesus was only human, after all. *Only* human? Could I say that? How could the Word of God be truly a man? One of the few verses I'd memorized at Bible school moved to the front of my brain, as if to answer my question. Jesus "didn't consider equality with God something to be grasped, but made himself nothing, taking the very nature of a servant, being made in human likeness." (Philippians 2:7, 8)

He was born a Jew. He had to learn the language that was spoken around him. Jesus was a child of his culture.

A delicate white butterfly meandered through the air along the edge of the track. I continued my pace, watching.

Here comes another one.

Timing its flight speed perfectly, the butterfly flitted across my path, two feet in front of my waist. I laughed out loud. A curiously common event, God spoke to me regularly through these butterflies playing chicken with me. I thought of them as miniature reminders of his playfully precise Spirit weaving along my life's path.

I finished the first lap. My scalp prickled and beads of sweat began to collect in my baseball cap. I distractedly rocked the cap back and forth on my head as a scratching tool. Droplets were released to run forward off my nose and fall into the ancient layers of Roman dust.

"I was sent only to the lost sheep of Israel." Why did he say that? John the Baptist had said Jesus was "the lamb of God who takes away the sin of the world."

I let my mind settle on another scripture about Jesus that said he was tempted in every way, just like me, without any extra advantage except that he didn't sin. I can't read minds. I don't carry around the knowledge of all time and creation. I'm limited by a weak memory and trapped traveling linearly through time. Same as Jesus was, or it wouldn't be true that we were tempted the same.

The difference was in the sinning.

Since Jesus didn't sin, he had nothing to interfere with the constantly maintained presence of God in his life. He always chose to do what God wanted him to do. He was so immersed in prayer that he could hear God's voice directing him. Nothing kept God from speaking directly to Jesus through the Holy Spirit, on a moment-to-moment basis. God gave Jesus knowledge and authority to act in his power, as needed. He was able to know the hearts of men because they were revealed to Jesus on the fly, providing the means to fulfill God's will. In effect, Jesus acted as the hand of God and spoke with God's words because of his receptivity and complete obedience.

I wondered if I could obey God so faithfully. Would he allow me to hear his voice as clearly as Jesus had? Could he give me that kind of power to follow his will?

"I was sent only to the lost sheep of Israel."

What if God chose *that particular moment* to reveal to Jesus that his ministry extended beyond the tribe of Israel by prompting him to heal this Gentile girl? He had to overcome the prejudices that surrounded him. I was tempted in the same way: to think of my own culture as superior. Jesus could relate to my culture shock. He sympathized with me.

Pfff... pff... pf... My footfalls changed their cadence as I slowed to a walk. My body had run the three laps, barely noticed by my internal complaints department. I continued walking another lap to catch my breath and cool down. Snails clung to the tall weeds among the ruins by the thousands, reminding me of salt water barnacles on ferry dock pilings back home. Sitting on the beach was another place I felt close to God.

I diverted from the open track and wandered beneath arched supports of the crumbling aqueduct and onto the Roman road. Once fitted and smooth, the groomed stones now succumbed to wear and weather. I sat down on the remnant of a marble pillar, cut down in its prime. I could have rested in the shade of the towering triumphal arch to my right, but I wanted to look at it. The space beneath the arch alone must have extended to a height of forty feet. The architecture of this formal entry portal into the city of Tyre exuded Roman flamboyance. The gateway I was looking at was the same gateway Jesus would have entered through. The same stones I stepped on, Jesus did, too.

"Jesus withdrew to the region of Tyre." The Bible never specifically said that Jesus entered Tyre, but by faith I *knew* that Jesus had been there in that place that I was sitting. He grew up in Nazareth, only thirty-five miles away, in the home of a carpenter. As the firstborn son, wouldn't he have gone to buy wood in the place that was famous for Lebanese cedar?

I imagined my setting as it would have been: a hub of the Roman Empire, bustling with traffic. Phoenician trade performed at a fever pitch. Amidst the frenzy walked a humble Jewish teenager, leading a donkey and cart overloaded with lumber. An interesting shadow was cast as he walked by carrying an extra beam over his shoulders.

The abrasive limestone scraped my leg as I got up. Jesus was also solid, real. I loved coming to the hippodrome because it reminded me so.

Time to go and drink some tea with Mustafa and ask him if he ever heard that Jesus healed a child in the neighborhood. It might be Noon before I get home to shower.

Hello All,

God is worthy of all our worship in every situation. We are choosing to glorify him and call out to him in our time of trouble. Your care for us has been a great encouragement.

We have already said that we plan to move in the event of a sure ceasefire, but we are now unsure if we could do that since we are hearing that most of the roads have been rendered impassible. We have 4x4 on the Mitsubishi Pajero that we are driving, but I am Imagining lots of debris and craters. I guess we'll have to depend on whatever cleanup and construction crews can improvise.

Our neighbor Kamel has been watching the newscasts on TV. He says that every bridge or road with sand below it has been destroyed, all over Lebanon. On the other hand, a lot of people have headed north in their cars and are not coming back. A few of our friends have called us to confirm that they've made it to Beirut after only a couple of hours of scary driving. We don't know what to think.

Last night was relatively quiet except for three or four loud blasts beyond the al-Bass Palestinian camp, in Bourj Shmelli, a nearby suburb. We are about 12 blocks away from there.

Today we're also going to gather with our group to pray, worship, and talk through potential plans for the coming days. There aren't a lot of options, but we do want to move together in whatever we need to do. We haven't decided yet whether we will come back to our house or stay with Edmond's family after the meeting. No one can tell "which place is safer" right now.

Many of you with practical military experience are sending good advice about survival tactics. We appreciate you. There seems to be general support for the course of action we have decided to take. Waiting.

Salaam,

Nate

HELICOPTERS AND TRIREMES

On a rare free Saturday morning, I took a break from studying Arabic and spent the time researching more about the history of my adopted home. Tyre used to be an island. She had a seafaring legacy. Since the days of King Hiram, an ally of the Hebrew King Solomon, the Phoenicians who founded Tyre were unparalleled in the skill of nautical trade. They devised the first phonetic alphabet and built a culture worthy of international commerce with powerful neighbors: Persians, Egyptians, Hebrews, and Greeks. Roughly circular in shape, Tyre was surrounded by water, four hundred yards from the mainland. Stone walls began at the water line and towered thirteen stories high. Two ports must have looked like broken teeth in the walls on the north and south sides.

Trading ships would arrive at the southern port loaded with merchandise and travel along a canal, which had been cut between the ports. As they inched along through the city, they could be unloaded at receiving stations and continue on to be loaded with new inventory before exiting quickly from the northern port.

Cargo ships would be accompanied at sea by 120 foot trireme warships, powered by two large, square sails and 170 oarsmen, arranged in three vertical layers. Stretched across the mouth of each port was an elaborate defensive system of chains that could be raised to prevent enemy vessels from entering.

Tyre was world famous for its temple to the god Melkert. From an opening in the wall facing the sea, the temple's altar was flanked by two massive pillars. One of the supports was made of gold and the other was said to be glowing emerald, which may have been made from the green tinted Phoenician glass, lighted from within like a lighthouse.

My apartment was a block away from the temple ruins. I stood on my balcony, coffee cup in hand, and tried to picture how impressive it had once been. The recessed dig had been abandoned in mid project. Three great pillars had been re-erected, but others lay scattered like cordwood among the edges of partial buildings jutting this way and that. The two-city-block-sized pit had been dug down to resemble preparations for building the foundation of a skyscraper, with a fence around its edge at street level to protect pedestrians from falling in. Unlike the better-developed historical sites around the Phoenician island, the temple was only accessible visually from the edges. I scanned the full scene from my balcony perch.

Then I saw it.

The gate was open and unattended. I had never seen it open before. I scrambled to make the most of this opportune moment to get in there and touch, where most tourists would never be allowed entry. I gulped down the rest of my coffee, grabbed my camera, and ran down the stairs and out of my building.

Snaking through the streets on the ground, I passed by the chain-link fence around the *City Ruins*, a nearby archeological site I had often visited. It was open for business, but not busy. The ticket taker in his booth watched TV and smoked cigarettes.

Most of that site's best-preserved treasures had been moved to the Lebanese National Museum in Beirut, but there were plenty of leftovers – either too big to move, or not perfect enough. Byzantine Christian tombs, a Roman aqueduct, even the remains of a Phoenician glassworks were unearthed, revealing the secrets of Tyre's colorful past.

As I neared the open gate, my opportunity for exploration didn't feel like as good an idea as it had from my balcony. Respect for the ancient, combined with the fear of getting caught trespassing, made me pause. I tried to look nonchalant and glanced around to see if anyone was watching. A compelling sense of holiness overcame my normal timidity. Slinking around wasn't possible anyway. As I descended below street level, I would be visible to anyone walking by or looking down from the neighborhood buildings. I started down the path from the gate boldly, as if I owned the place. But as I approached what remained of the buildings, my footfalls took on a light reverence. Here were layers of religion.

I felt small. Time loomed over me, feeling like a tower that dwarfed my stubby lifespan. Empires were born and buried in Tyre. Yet, somehow I had become entangled in her story and was humbled by the impact of touching the eternal.

Phoenician Melkert worship had given way to Christianity. A cathedral of pink marble was eventually built over the site of the pagan temple. The transition wasn't peaceful. Followers of The Way lost their lives for their faith in Jesus at the Arena in Tyre, a block away. The church father Origen was buried in the cathedral of Tyre after dying from wounds he received while being tortured.

After Constantine adopted Christianity as the state religion, Tyre became a seat of ecclesiastical power. Bishop Paulinus and Eusebius of Caesarea convened the first church council in Tyre to discuss a new controversy called Arianism and to discern the orthodox understanding of the divine and human natures of Jesus. The council's findings were later overturned by the creators of the Athanasian Creed.

Saracen invaders sparked the Crusades before the turning of the first millennium. Still a formidable fortress, Tyre would prove a resistant prize for both European Crusaders and Muslim resistance forces. This very cathedral hosted the coronation ceremonies of European Crusaders being crowned king of Jerusalem. Alternatively, it served as a mosque as often as the city changed hands between Muslim and Christian armies.

The path I followed ended, but I continued on amidst the dusty rubble. At one place the ground dipped and I walked below a massive horizontal pillar suspended by mounds of earth on either side. It reminded me of walking under a fallen Douglas fir log, spanning a ravine in the woods back home. I reached over my head to let my fingers graze its still smooth surface, contrasting the feeling with my thoughts of rough tree bark. The honking, busy bustle of the modern city around me faded from my consciousness.

Alexander the Great once stood here.

Alexander came to town in 332 BC on his way to conquering the Persian Empire. His land invasion around the Mediterranean included a crucial strategy of conquering every seaport, clear down through Egypt. There couldn't be a single point along the coast where the Persian nautical fleet would be able to supply a counterforce to cut off his supply lines and attack him from the rear as he advanced inland. The only port city that had the nerve to resist him was Tyre.

Tyre's god was also Alexander's personal deity. Melkert was the Phoenician version of the Greek Heracles that Alexander venerated in his native Macedonia. It may have seemed like an obvious opportunity for a partnership, but the Tyrians denied Alexander's demand to be allowed entry to worship their common god.

On the mainland coast, opposite the southern port of the island, the invading armies camped at an ancient spring and founded a new city named Alexandrina. They had already destroyed the small Phoenician city there, directly east of the island and north of the spring. Alexander ordered one work crew to begin the construction of a thirteen-story, wheeled siege-tower. Another team set to work creating a land-bridge by throwing the remains of ruined buildings into the sea. The builders were bombarded by fireballs from above and attacked from the water by sailors, who could advance swiftly in trireme ships from the ports and then retreat to safety.

My surroundings snapped back into focus as I met the gaze of a passerby on the outside edge of the fence along the road. *Best not to push my luck. I'd better get out of here.* Though he couldn't have cared less, I gave the guy a look that said, "I was just leaving," and moved toward the exit.

Once more on the street, I wasn't yet ready to go home. I wanted to check out something else. I worked my way to the southern facing beach that ran along the peninsula Alexander created. The land bridge he started was widened by more than two thousand years of sedimentary deposits.

From a slightly elevated vantage point, I looked south in the direction that the shoreline took as it hooked westerly toward the border with Israel. Alexander's camp at the spring in Alexandrina was visible to me in the form of the Rashedieh Palestinian camp, which had taken its place. On my left, the coastal edge of tall apartment buildings mimicked the city walls that existed in antiquity. In the center of this natural bay, the final naval battle took place with triremes clashing in the waves, just out of bow range from the walls.

Alexander enlisted the help of the rival Phoenician trading city of Sidon, which had already surrendered to him. The Sidonian fleet attacked from the seaward side as Alexander coordinated the landward thrust and broke through Tyre's walls.

Thirty thousand women and children were sold into slavery and two thousand men of Tyre were nailed to crosses along the beach to die of asphyxiation from the pressure of the weight of their bodies on their chests. After seven months of laying siege, Alexander finally went in to worship at the altar of his pagan god.

The world shook in fear from news of the fall of Tyre and the brutality of its conqueror. His punishment for resistance was such a harsh example that many cities would submit to him without fighting back.

The cleansing Mediterranean removed all trace of the carnage. Much is forgotten in the passage of time. I shuffled through the sand about the distance of six or seven blocks to see the evidence of more recent events.

The previous week, I had been hanging laundry on the drying lines on my balcony – much to the amusement of the giggly neighbor girls who hadn't seen a man hang laundry before. A not too distant explosion compressed the air. The windows rattled behind me from the impact of the roaring sound waves. I went inside and made calls to learn what had happened. It wasn't long before Mustafa was relaying what he'd seen.

He had been heading toward his rental apartment facing the sea, when he heard the thumping of rotor blades and looked over the water as an Israeli Apache Helicopter approached. It slowed to hover before firing. The first missile struck the water close to the shore, but the second found its way to a flat in an apartment building. Then the helicopter turned and darted away as abruptly as it had arrived.

In the Israeli news, it was reported as an attack on a Hezbollah naval observation post, but Red Cross volunteers immediately responding to the scene said no evidence was found that suggested it was anything other than a domestic residence. No one was in the apartment at the time, but several neighbors were hospitalized for injuries.

I arrived at the building to survey the damage from below on the street. From my angle I could see the gaping square hole on the front of the fourth floor flat. The incident hadn't disrupted the normal social flow of life. Unexpected military events happen in Lebanon from time to time, just like tornadoes in Kansas.

I turned back to where the helicopter had fired from over the sea – about the same place that I always imagined the ancient Macedonian-Phoenician skirmishes happening. I wondered what would have happened if those Phoenicians had simply surrendered to Alexander when he first arrived.

The Phoenicians were no strangers to invasion. A steady stream of conquerors had come and gone along this spit of land that has connected three continents from the beginning of recorded history. In most cases the Phoenicians integrated with the earlier invaders, sometimes greatly increasing their commerce from the added diversity. But this time they resisted and the pride of independence led to their destruction. How might I apply this ancient lesson to the current Lebanese resistance movement? Were battles for nationalistic superiority damaging Lebanon more than independence could ever benefit them? Could I suggest to my Shia friends that more advantage could be found in assimilating with Tyre's current occupiers?

I decided it was best to keep my thoughts to myself. The comparison wasn't a fair one anyway. There were major differences between the powerful Phoenician city-state and the relative insignificance of Tyre's current standing. These Tyrians had never tasted power. They fought simply for the right to live out their lives with acceptable levels of persecution from their own government.

By the time I arrived in Tyre, the Israeli occupation was eighteen years old. Long years of resistance built muscle and discipline. Hezbollah's power was Israel's own creation. In the spring of 2000, I had become part of the story of Tyre. I was included in the big picture, but no longer saw myself as the center of the universe. I'd gained perspective of my place, but still expectantly awaited a relevant part to play.

Alexander was here… and Nate.

From: Nate Scholz
Sent: Sunday, July 16, 2006
Subject: Day 5 — Evening

Dear Family and Friends,

This has been one of the longest and most difficult days in my life. As you have no doubt heard, there was more activity in the city of Tyre.

We went to Edmond's house thinking that we would stay there until we heard it was safe to head north to Beirut and beyond. However, about an hour after we arrived we were shaken by four massive bombardments that struck a building next to the hospital only half a block away from where we were. The four-story building was leveled and ours was shaken. We decided that there may be other targets in the area that we didn't know about and the three families packed up to move again.

We came back into the city to stay at the vacant flat of some British friends who are vacationing in England. We feel it is safest since it is on the second floor, set back from the sea, and surrounded by taller buildings. We also have neighbors here whom we know and trust. We are about four blocks away from our own house.

We heard a rumor that the Rest House Hotel & Resort is putting up folks with foreign passports until their governments are able to organize some way to help them. Denis and I went to investigate, but it was all talk.

On the way back, we stopped at my apartment and took some cushions to sleep on and more food and water. While we were there, jets dropped messages written in Arabic warning folks to stay away from Hezbollah-related places. We should have taken a hint from that of what was coming next.

About thirty minutes later, the Israelis hit a building on the edge of town, about five blocks from us, where Naomi used to go to preschool. That blast also shook our building and rattled the glass. Shrapnel fell near our car. The children are still disturbed.

There are twelve of us sharing two small bedrooms and one bathroom. Currently, we are out of running water and there is no electricity, but we are all together and safe, though growing increasingly weary. We're having endless discussions of which location is safer and where we should move next, but I think we are staying put here until there is conclusive information that will ensure a safe escape.

Our neighbors have offered to share their food stores with us and have been very hospitable. The population of the city has swelled because of people fleeing from the surrounding villages, and there are many people out in the streets discussing the events. Children are playing. Life goes on.

We can still hear distant shelling, but compared to the nearer teeth-rattling ones that we experienced today, we can almost ignore them completely.

Please pray for our mental stability and to continue to exhibit Jesus-following behavior amongst ourselves and with our neighbors. At times like these our testimony is sometimes tested. I am glad to report, however, that our faith is standing firm in our savior, no matter what happens.

God bless you with peace... and us.

Salaam,

Nate

A TIME TO MOURN

Sadiq and I were finishing an Arabic lesson when I asked, "Why is everyone wearing black today?"

"We're mourning the death of Hussein," Sadiq said. He was referring to the Shia community to which he belonged, which made up about 90% of Tyre's population. He continued, "I'm going to a majlis later today at the mosque. Why don't you come with me?"

"What's a *majlis*?" I asked.

"It's a recitation of the history of the Karbala massacre. There are daily meetings in the week leading up to the day of Ashura."

I was nervous about how the community would tolerate a white Westerner barging into such an intensely intimate expression of their culture. I didn't want to be disruptive, but I *did* want to understand the passions of local society.

"I don't have any black clothes," I tested.

He waved his hand dismissively, "That doesn't matter. It's nothing."

I seriously doubted it was nothing. From what I'd seen walking to class that morning, I thought a law had been passed overnight, commanding everyone to wear only black. But when would I get an invitation like this again – to experience this kind of meeting firsthand with a friend by my side to explain what was happening?

"Okay, let's go!" I grinned. "Can you tell me more about the story in advance?"

The day was called *Ashura*, Sadiq explained, which meant "tenth" in Arabic because it fell annually on the tenth day of the Islamic month of Muharram.

After Mohammed died, conflict arose among his followers over who should lead the movement. Some believed the spiritual leadership should be passed down through descendants of Mohammed as in a monarchy. They were pitted against those who wanted to elect successors from powerful tribal chiefs and governors, to rule a Muslim civil and religious domain, called a *caliphate*.

Mohammed himself never gave any specific directions either way about his successors. The crucial division point took place in 680 AD in the Iraqi valley of Karbala.

Yazid, the son of the Syrian Governor, represented the caliphate in the battle. Those who found themselves on this side of the war developed the Sunni tradition: those who *follow the traditions of the prophet*. The Shia, or *people of the household*, were of the clan of Mohammed and followed the prophet's grandson, Hussein.

A majority of Muslims had already sworn allegiance to Yazid. When Hussein refused to submit, few safe havens remained available for his family. They crossed the desert together from Mecca to a promising town called Kufa. Their caravan was ambushed on the way by a detachment of four thousand soldiers from Yazid's army. Access to the water of the nearby Euphrates River was cut off, and the enemy weakened them through thirst for a week before attacking. Hussein's defensive force consisted of thirty-two horsemen and forty soldiers on foot. As the battle ensued, Hussein and his men moved away from the camp to minimize danger to the women and children from the rain of arrows. Hussein's fighters fought valiantly to protect their spiritual leader, but they were too greatly outnumbered. After the bodyguard were killed, Hussein's sons and other family members came out from the camp to join in the fighting. One by one they were cut down.

None were left to fight. Hussein advanced alone on his horse and sustained multiple injuries before being knocked to the ground as a stone struck his head. An arrow pierced him in the chest and he yanked it out himself. The enemy encircled him, but waited.

In Hussein's last moments a voice came from heaven, "We are satisfied with your deeds and sacrifices."

Hussein sheathed his sword and bowed to pray. As his forehead touched the ground, an enemy soldier cut his head from his body.

The many gory details of the story were passed down from that day by Hussein's sister Zainab to the following Shia generations. Hussein's sickly son Ali and his cousin Hassan were the only surviving males to carry on the bloodline of Mohammed.

Shia Muslims have a motto of suffering, "The victory of blood over the sword." They believe that Hussein's obedience to God until death, standing up for the truth, earned him a position as an intercessor. His sacrifice won God's favor for his community.

In the West, we've gotten out of the habit of wearing black to show we're mourning. Sometimes people wear black armbands or simply choose darker colors. Not so in Tyre during the observance of Ashura. With few exceptions, people wore solid black from head to toe.

My Shia neighbors took their mourning seriously. They turned off the booming car stereos that usually filled the streets with Middle Eastern pop music. All I heard were the chanted dirges, played over an outdoor loudspeaker by the owner of the video store down the street. If Ashura coincided with a birthday, the party would be skipped. People refrained from laughter. Purchases of anything new were delayed. The local movie theater closed down. Even the children played in a subdued attitude. Clearly, Ashura was a time for somber reflection. That year, it was also a time of sweating.

Occasionally, in the springtime, the wind would change direction and our normally pleasant seventy to eighty degree weather would be hijacked by Saudi heat and humidity.

Sadiq and I slowly walked the few blocks from my house to join the crowd of men filing into the high ceilinged *Hossinieh*. This multi-purpose community building connected to the main Shia mosque close to the market. I was the only non-Arab, non-Muslim in the room that I could tell. We chose a place on the left side of the room beside a pillar, which offered me a bit of cover to retain my anonymity. A sea of white plastic chairs were occupied and adjusted, with vibrating sounds as they scraped on the marble floor.

I whispered questions into Sadiq's ear. "Women don't come to these meetings?"

"Women have their own *majlis* meetings in homes. Only men go to the mosque," he replied.

I motioned with my head to the front of the room, "Why do those guys up front have different colored turbans?"

He was so patient in explaining things. He said, "Those are sheikhs, our religious leaders. The white turbans are for the normal sheikhs, but black ones are reserved for those who are descended from the prophet, *the Sayyideen*."

The local Shia clergy sat in couches of honor along the front wall. Occasionally another sheikh would show up and they all stood and greeted the newcomer in the customary round of hand-shaking and the triple cheek kiss. Left-right-left. Then everybody shifted to allow the new one to sit in the location his status dictated. They all wore heavy layered black robes that looked stiflingly hot. Sweat dripped off their long black beards. Ceiling fans turned lazily overhead. I expected the concrete walls to start dripping from the heavy humidity.

Men continued to drift in as the mosque administrator introduced the guest cantor, who had traveled from Iraq to chant the section of the story of Hussein that we would be listening to that afternoon. He began with some introductory comments, alternating between shouting and chanting in the formal Arabic style that was completely different from the conversational Arabic that I was learning.

At the beginning, Sadiq occasionally whispered an abbreviated translation of the speech, but the volume level made it impossible to continue. Without understanding, I had a hard time staying focused. I let my eyes wander across the posters hanging on the wall, each with a screen printed likeness of Imam Musa Sadr. Sadiq had already told me his story. He was an influential leader in the 1970s who had charmed southern Lebanese of all faiths into living at peace with each other before his mysterious disappearance in Libya.

The heat got to me and my concentration was fading when a change in the action caught my attention. The cantor had moved from his introductory formalities into chanting the story of the massacre. In between sentences he now began to catch his breath in a sob. I thought, *Oh brother, that's cheesy.* I looked around expecting to see men rolling their eyes at each other, but was surprised to see most heads bowed. Every now and then a guy would be rocking to himself or shaking his head with eyes closed, or wiping a tear. *Wow. They're taking this pretty seriously.* Sadiq sniffled as the preacher continued in earnest, his voice cracked with emotion. I kept my eyes forward, conscious of the ripple of emotion that escalated around me. *What is going on here?*

I found myself doubting everyone's sincerity. Maybe they had some way of making themselves cry on demand. Where were the buckets of minced onions?

By the time the cantor finished, the four hundred men in the room with me were sobbing and shedding streams of tears, wailing, "Oh, Hussein!" Mine were the only dry eyes. I was stunned at Sadiq's authentic release of emotions. How often does one experience a crowded room of crying men?

Easter was just a week away. I imagined what it would be like to be in a church with men weeping like that for Jesus on Good Friday.

***

In 2000, the tenth day of Muharram in the Islamic Calendar fell on April 15. On that day of Ashura, busloads of people arrived from throughout the South and converged on the streets of Tyre to remember it together. It wasn't a parade, though it had all of the same elements except the sentiment of celebration. A better term was "processional."

I leaned against the trunk of a slim tree along the street to observe. Its shade provided some relief from the heat. I had purchased a black shirt since the *majlis* meeting with Sadiq, and the dark fabric was baking me. I didn't know how the other folks with me on the sidewalk could stand it in the sun, never mind the superhuman endurance shown by those who marched. I imagined that the organizers of the processional had purposefully planned it for the hottest part of the day to magnify the empathizing effect for the plight of Hussein.

The participants initially gathered and organized at a staging ground, down in the market parking lot by the port. The processional moved onto Bank Street, led by a flatbed truck with six-foot tall speakers mounted on its frame. Poetic chanting blared from the speakers along with a drumbeat that sounded like the cracking of a stick hitting the edge of a snare drum. When the truck reached the main crowds of onlookers, where I leaned against my tree, the recording was turned off. A white-bearded sheikh in robes sat on a tall-backed, wooden chair in the back of the truck. He began to chant. He shouted into the microphone until his voice strained. I heard an army marching behind, but the powerful rhythmic sound it produced wasn't coming from pounding boots.

Sweating men lined up in formation and sectioned off in groups of about a hundred, with a gap of twenty feet or so between groups. They stepped barefoot on searing-hot asphalt, steadily moving forward to the beat of the drum. Their bodies swayed back and forth slightly, so that on every fourth step they could rhythmically swing their right arms up and bring their hands pounding against their chests. It was this sound that overpowered the softer step of their feet.

... *pad, pad, pad, WHUMP, pad, pad, pad, WHUMP...*

As the sheer number of them continued on, and the truck went into the distance, the drumbeat was lost in the sound of the beating of palm to chest. They took turns repeating the dirge-like chanting of the leader. The sheikh disappeared from view when the truck turned onto Abou Deeb Street, but the sound of his voice was relayed through successive truckloads of speakers.

After every few hundred marchers, a parade float displayed some gruesome depiction of the massacre story. I also saw political floats that associated Israel with the enemy armies of Yazid. One artist's depiction condemned the *Great Satan* of the United States. The American flag was reproduced with skulls where the stars should have been. The red and white stripes became the contrails of bombs that had fallen on them.

I couldn't help but be impressed at the thousands of men who were there, and then the women came in equal numbers, some with babes-in-arms, representing the women and children of Hussein's camp. Helpers along the side of the road brought some relief from the heat by spraying water on those in the procession to cool them down. The women didn't walk barefoot in formation, but they did produce the same cadence of chest beating as the men.

At the tail of the flow of bodies were waves of uniformed boys and girls in scout packs, marching on behalf of the numerous small villages in the rolling hills between Nabatieh and Tyre that make up the Lebanese Shia heartland.

Something in me was drawn to this unifying theology of suffering. The sorrow of those days of remembrance each year was the tie that bound the Shia community together. I recoiled from the dark pre-occupation with death and gore, but sweetness also came from the comfort of a community mourning together. My faith was strengthened by their example of devotion.

After the last float passed by, the crowds dissipated and I headed for home. I passed by Mustafa in his shop, and I had to laugh when I saw him. He'd stayed at work during the event, and it was a good thing he had. He'd chosen to wear a white shirt, white pants, and white shoes as his own belligerent way of resisting the Shia majority around him. He was a Sunni, and everyone knew it.

The Sunni culture is one of victory. The idea of strength through suffering is alien to them. Defeat provides no honor. The conquering armies of Yazid had passed leadership through the caliphs of the Umayyad Dynasty and beyond into successive Muslim empires.

The day I first observed an Ashura processional was one of the largest turnouts and the best prepared it had been for years. Hezbollah flexed its resistance muscles, causing Israelis to question their resolve to remain in the occupied zone. The thousands of men who marched that day recognized the pride of standing up in their own battle for righteousness against the Jewish occupier. Each one remembered the suffering and loss he had personally experienced, garnished with the solidarity of the lost Imam, Hussein.

From: Nate Scholz
Sent: Monday, July 17, 2006
Subject: Day 6 — Morning

Things are looking bad in the news. We have weighed our risks and believe that we should join a convoy heading north. Many vehicles have made it to Beirut, so it's apparently possible.

We will go to the Rest House Resort and try to hire a taxi driver to lead us on whatever roads are known to be open.

We are leaving right now at 9:00 AM. I pray that we will send an update from some safe place before most of you have read this message.

Pray for us.

Salaam,

Nate

FATIMA GATE AND BEYOND

"Just like that? They're gone?"

Sadiq and I walked in the street. The mood around us was charged with astonishment. People clustered, buzzed.

"Yeah. The resistance chased them out in only two days," he said.

On May 24, Israel had announced its intentions to de-occupy Lebanon. They planned to withdraw in a staged retreat, covered by their hired Lebanese Christian militia. Alarmed at the thought of being abandoned to the vengeance of their fellow Lebanese, the South Lebanon Army refused to further condemn themselves by cooperating. Israel had little choice but to leave immediately, so they destroyed their hardened concrete bunkers with explosives to render them unusable, and they left.

We neared my apartment and stopped to check in with Mustafa at his shop.

"Peace to you," we greeted.

"And to you, peace." Mustafa was already repositioning chairs and calling for tea from the neighboring café. "Sit! Drink tea."

We sat and drank – no need to fill Mustafa in on what we were talking about. The conversation was the same everywhere in the country.

Sadiq said, "Israel has controlled the South for eighteen years, since I was six. I don't remember ever being in that part of my own country, and it's only a few miles from here."

South Lebanon had been occupied for Sadiq's entire life. Armed Palestinians already controlled the area when Sadiq was born. Yasir Arafat had managed to relocate his Palestinian Liberation Organization (PLO) to Lebanon after King Hussein kicked them out of Jordan. With a little help from the PLO, the Lebanese civil war started in Beirut in the late 1970s, which tied up the Lebanese Army and gave the PLO free reign to execute their attacks on Northern Israel. They were not fighting from a country they thought of as "home," and were unconcerned with any danger they created for Lebanese civilians in the form of Israeli reprisals. Weapons availability made life in Tyre like living in the American Wild West.

Israel saw that Lebanon couldn't prevent the PLO from attacking them, so in 1982 General Arial Sharon was authorized to invade Lebanon and eliminate the threat to Israeli borders.

In Tyre, the Lebanese were caught in the crossfire between the foreign forces among them. Israeli Jews and the Palestinian Sunnis were the latest in a long line of oppressors who used Lebanese homes and shops and land as the stage for a war over which the local Shia had no power.

Curfews kept locals off city streets after dark and the Israelis patrolled to enforce it. Originally, the southern residents had been happy to see the Israelis gain control over the armed Palestinian thugs that had tormented them.

The Palestinians were disarmed and the Israelis withdrew to a ten-mile wide swath of land along their border. This region took on the regular title of "Occupied Zone." When the Israelis pulled out of the city of Tyre, the Shia massacred many Palestinian refugees in retribution for causing the Israeli invasion. No one was innocent in this story. Each party committed atrocities.

Tyre was a fifteen-minute walk north of the first Israeli checkpoint. Those wanting to pass the guard post had to prove their residency. When it became clear that the Israelis were simply going to replace the Palestinians as foreign occupiers, the sentiment changed. They had worn out their welcome.

A Lebanese resistance force formed as a grassroots movement among the Lebanese Shia living in or near this occupied zone. Regular people organized themselves and fought back. Two distinct groups arose. Amal was financed and supplied by Syria and inclined toward negotiating political solutions. Hezbollah was equipped by Iran and preferred armed resistance. The angry fighters flocking to the new militias lived amidst the concrete bunkers the occupiers built. The freedom and safety of their wives, children, neighbors, homes, shops and farms were at stake.

In the summer of 1982, when Israel finally responded to the Palestinian raids by invading, I was finishing my sophomore year of high school and was more concerned about when the next Scorpions album would come out than what was happening in the country of Lebanon. *Such different lives we'd lived, my friends and I. How did I get here?*

I looked over at Mustafa. He wore a big impulsive grin and said, "Let's go tomorrow."

"Hunh?" I honked. I instantly regretted making that stupid American sound we use when we're confused or didn't hear.

He continued, "Nate has a car. We can tour around the South to the border and see for ourselves what's happening. This is an important moment in history."

"Can we do that so soon?" I worried. "I mean, can we just drive in there and nobody will stop us?"

Sadiq was on board. "Mustafa is right. We have to take this opportunity. We'll just go and see how far we can get."

"Cool. Let's go for it." We agreed to leave first thing in the morning. I filled the gas tank and wished I had air conditioning.

The same idea we had was sparked in the minds of citizenry all over Lebanon, as half the population made plans for a road trip.

We started south along the ten-mile stretch of formerly occupied coast on a pilgrimage to witness Lebanon's liberation firsthand. Abandoned ports and coast guard stations made for a ghost-town effect. We left early enough that traffic was still fairly sparse, so we were free to pull over and stop for photo ops. A gigantic, colorful billboard had been erected in the middle of nowhere alongside the road, hand illustrated by artists with the message "Thanks,

Hezbollah." The day grew hotter and our path rose from sea level along the ridge of limestone cliffs. Fishermen stood ankle-deep in the distant shallows below with their long poles.

At Naqoura, we could not go any farther south without running into the freshly sealed border gate. We turned left and drove up into the beleaguered villages. The people had come out of their run-down buildings to sit on plastic chairs and watch the parade drive by. They had kept their gardens up. Thousands of red roses stood out, vibrant against the grey, cracked concrete walls. A steady stream of buses and cars flowed where Israeli armored patrols had passed the day before. The residents must have wondered where all these friends had been when they needed them over the past two decades.

Flags fluttered in the visitors' wake: Lebanese cedars, Hezbollah yellow, and Amal green. Sightseers ate the food they had brought along and threw the wrappers out their windows.

"Turn here," Mustafa said. "I think I know where the commander was killed." I followed his directions and veered onto a quiet side road, departing from the already thickening traffic. After a few minutes of driving, we discovered an abandoned military compound in the middle of a field, without a single tree or shrub for miles.

We got out and walked around until we smelled the half-decayed remains of a dead dog in a ditch – it looked like a German shepherd. In the wire fence ringing the yard was a blackened hole. We stood a short distance from a deserted concrete building. Mustafa scanned the scrubland beyond the fence. "Where did the Hezbollah guy hide?" he wondered.

The resistance had years to perfect their techniques. Israeli military bases were fixed targets on Lebanese soil. Hezbollah fighters planted bombs in stealth by night and occasionally fired rockets. The Israelis responded with an iron fist to the loss of Israeli life. They took prisoners and restricted movement, eliminating hope for a normal life and heightening the locals' felt need to resist. Hezbollah and Amal collected donations from Shia around Lebanon and began to financially help Muslims in the Occupied Zone who had lost their livelihood and couldn't feed their families. No one else was helping them so they helped themselves.

When the security zone was sealed off from the rest of Lebanon, the impoverished minority Christian inhabitants in the South were isolated. The Israelis enlisted many Christian men into a proxy army, using desperation to turn neighbor against neighbor. These men became known as the South Lebanon Army, though they had no connection with the government of Lebanon.

In January, a stealthy resistance fighter had planted a bomb by night next to the fence we now stood by, then patiently waited until the commander of the Western Brigade of the South Lebanon Army was within range before manually detonating the charge. The German shepherd was shot and left by the retreating soldiers because it failed to do its job and sniff out the bomb. We followed the events close enough to commemorate the story by shooting the dog again – this time with our cameras. We recorded evidence of an incident that was a trigger for Israeli withdrawal. This lonely place had played its role in history and then returned to obscurity.

Mustafa noticed Sadiq wandering. "Don't go too far away. There are land mines everywhere, you know?"

We rejoined the stream of traffic. The road strayed and returned to proximity with the border in loping curves. We paused again along tobacco fields and I took a photo of Mustafa and Sadiq holding the Lebanese flag between them with Israel visible in the background. Roadside thistles caught my attention. Maybe because of the activity of the day, I waxed philosophical on how they symbolized what South Lebanon had become to Israel: the beautiful hot pink flower fixed atop the thick, spike-covered stalk – alluring, yet dangerous.

We next approached the village of Kfar Killa, which was the focal point of everyone's journey that day. The road paralleled the border fence closest there, and the Israeli town of Metulla sat just across the border. I was soon to respect the unforeseen danger of our journey.

Traffic essentially stopped. Other pilgrims got out of their buses and milled around. I stopped the car's engine and restarted every five minutes to move forward a car length. At the rate we traveled, we needed to conserve fuel. The razor-wire-lined border fence crowded to the right, a foot away from the Honda's passenger door. An orchard lay to our left, likely loaded with land mines. The sense of being trapped in this precarious position converted our joyride into more of a stress-ride. If things got out of hand, we had nowhere to go – and things were threatening to get out of hand. A young man threw a fist-sized rock, breaking a glass cover to an overhead floodlight. Many more were giving Israel back the newly liberated land by hurling stony bits of Lebanon across the border. As an Israeli armored truck raced by on patrol, rocks hailed against its near side. Nothing would have kept the Israelis from returning fire with bullets, but they didn't slow down.

Within the mayhem, armed Hezbollah militiamen in black fatigues defied my expectations in their attempts to control the situation by yelling at the Lebanese civilians to calm down and stop throwing the rocks.

Probably not a coincidence, but the three of us chose this moment to need a lavatory – not good timing. We weren't going anywhere fast, let alone to a place with restroom facilities.

Surrounding us, a hundred people shared the road within easy sight. The only possibility for ducking out of sight to relieve ourselves was the orchard. Now we had three reasons to sweat: the heat of the day with no air-conditioning in the car, fear of death by stray bullets from pregnant rifles, and the prospect of spending the rest of the day in peed pants. Sadiq and Mustafa took their chances in the orchard, but I had to stay in the driver's seat. Neither of them could drive a stick shift. I was destined to suffer much.

We inched our way along the main road and temporarily away from the border. It took an hour to move a mile. When we eventually curved back to the border, we understood the reason for the delay. People parked here to walk down a blockaded access road for their chance to look at Fatima Gate. Miraculously, we found an open parking space and got out for a look. The crowds moved tightly with an unusual recipe of emotions: half a cup of joy, a pinch of fear, a dash of defiance.

Fatima Gate had been used as the key crossing point for Israeli vehicles between occupied Lebanon and Israel. After the Israelis left, this crossing point became their most vulnerable location. Their requirement to guard it closely made it an opportune place for regular Lebanese civilians to face the enemy Israelis, posted in defensive positions a few yards away. They longed to identify themselves with the victory of the resistance.

I was distracted by my own competing priority. A brief search yielded no open shops that might have a restroom. I continued to fidget and exercise my abdominal muscles as we took in the scene.

The mile-long access road stretched out before us, teeming with humanity. The gate was at the midway point, accessible only by pedestrians.

A middle-aged man collected rocks in a pile, and then sat expectantly on his haunches, waiting for the next plated Hummer to zoom by. It reminded me of the seasons described by Solomon in Ecclesiastes 3:5. "There is a time to scatter stones and a time to gather them, a time to embrace and a time to refrain from embracing."

We stood next to the stand of an ice-cream vendor, who also sold Hezbollah flag souvenirs. The top of his yellow-painted stand was decorated with a khaki-clad teddy bear and plastic replicas of the Russian Katyusha rockets used by Hezbollah.

"What are they looking at?" Sadiq asked us. A cluster of folks pointed at a patch of tall bushes ten feet beyond the fence on the other side of the border. Someone nearby overheard him.

"Look closely. It's an observation post. There are soldiers in there watching us."

I looked intently at the spot for a few minutes. I almost gave up, and then saw the head movement of an Israeli inside. I should have heard him *breathing* he was so close.

A sudden commotion broke my concentration. A surge pulsed through the crowd with a frenzy of yelling and news cameras jockeying for position. Sirens blared. Two men ran up the road, carrying a third. They each had an arm and a leg of a wounded man, who was floating forward, unconscious and suspended in a seated position, covered in blood. He somehow managed to get through the fence at the gate and had thrown rocks at the Israelis from their own side before being shot. The men whisked him past us and into an ambulance. A glance back at the crammed roads left me hoping for his sake there was a clinic nearby.

"I don't think we should go up to the gate." I said.

On our way back to the car, Sadiq stopped at a street vendor. He bought me a DVD with a collection of video news footage, outlining the occupation and Hezbollah's victory. He explained why he wanted me to have it.

"This will show you everything that has happened here. You can help explain it to your friends in America. I don't think they know."

Traffic out of Kfar Killa was tolerable, but still stop and go. We traveled slowly along the two-lane road choked with four lanes of vehicles taking turns cutting each other off in opposite directions. Putting some space between us and the border felt safer, but I was anything but relaxed. Stopping and going for hours on hills had taken a toll on my ankles and legs. They shook with the fatigue of operating the clutch and brake. I battled my bladder in waves. In brief breaks, the action subsided and then flared. I danced frantically in my seat, near tears, attempting to safely maneuver the car a foot at a time up a hill without rear-ending the car ahead.

The last on our list of places to stop was Khiam Prison. We had watched the first TV footage the day before. News cameras arrived with the first wave of rescuers, right after the abandonment of its keepers. It took awhile to get them out because the keys had not been left. Barred doors were torn apart and opened and the captives squinted into the sunlight.

The national wounds inflicted here would be slow to heal. Christian Lebanese traitors in the South Lebanon Army controlled the Khiam prison facility, directed by the Israeli military. As they retreated back to their own country, the Israelis offered two choices to their collaborators: live in refugee camps in northern Israel, or take their chances and stay in Lebanon. Many chose to stay when the Lebanese government offered them amnesty, but revenge could be exacted privately with a little patience and creativity.

"They interrogated me and then got instructions for torture by email," said one prisoner in an interview.

Local villagers shared stories, too. A Shia Muslim doctor explained what it was like to live in the shadow of the prison. "They would sometimes come to my house in the middle of the night and make me treat the wounds of a prisoner."

The smell hit us even before we reached the front gate, pulling my memory back to the removal of a cast on my arm when I was nine years old. *What was I going to see here?*

The three flags of the day flew proudly above the entrance up the hill we climbed from the parking lot. The crackle of over-taxed loudspeakers blared a dirge of Arabic chanting.

I was initially grateful for one thing about Khiam prison: it had a bathroom.

As I rejoined my friends in the courtyard, I began to take in the horror of my surroundings. My physical relief magnified a new feeling of emptiness.

The other witnesses among us drifted along rows of holding cells, soberly shaking their heads. Metal rings were fixed high in the walls of the courtyard. We recalled a prisoner's testimony that he was chained naked with his hands above his head, standing in shallow water while electrically charged battery cables were applied to his genitals.

We continued down a long corridor of cells inside. A grating in the ceiling provided just enough natural light to accentuate the disgusting conditions and hint at what couldn't be seen in the shadows.

Visiting the prison so early after its liberation afforded us the unsanitized view that later pilgrims would miss. For the first time that day, I felt conspicuous among the olive-complexioned folks around me. These Shia Muslims shared the solidarity of historical persecution.

We got back in the car and continued our trek.

The sun set shortly after clearing a particularly gnarled intersection, made worse because nobody knew which way to go. This was undiscovered territory for most of the drivers on the road. They didn't know the way home and neither did I.

"See that castle up there?" My eyes followed the direction of Mustafa's finger. I saw a jag on the summit of the hilly range, miles to the west.

"That's a castle?" I asked.

"It's Beaufort Castle, left over from the Crusades," he said. "Nabatieh is just over that crest, and then we'll get down to the coast road and back to Tyre."

The remainder of the drive was quiet. Sadiq and Mustafa slept. I passed a couple of hours just creeping up the switchbacks of the Lebanon Mountain range.

A snake-like line of red lights zigged ahead of me into the distance above, and the white lights below zagged on forever. The marathon of a hundred miles lasted twelve hours before I was home again and liberated to sleep.

From: Nate Scholz
Sent: Monday, July 17, 2006
Subject: Day 6 — Evening

Praise God!

We are still in Lebanon, but we are no longer in Tyre. We are at the Adma retreat center, which is also a Christian monastery, in the hills above Jounieh, north of Beirut.

We perceived that the trouble was going to continue to escalate and we realized how difficult it would be for our embassy to rescue us from Tyre, so we loaded our three families into two cars and left Tyre this morning, along with thousands of our Lebanese friends and neighbors who were also fleeing the city. We just arrived here at 5:00 PM after a tense seven-hour drive.

We waited at a traffic jam in a precarious place at the crossing for the Litani River, but made it through to Sidon. Then the bridge we wanted to go over must have been hit minutes before we got there. Cars came back from that road with people shouting to turn around and go back.

Instead, we made a circuitous route through the hills around Jezzine and then over to Beit Eddine. Finally we took a route through the Shouf Mountains to get here. The roads were crowded and we were happy to continue running into some of our neighbors along the way as well.

Now we are only a fifteen-minute drive away from the American embassy and we can stay here until they arrange for an evacuation. The Scholz family is definitely planning to evacuate when possible. Denis's family is currently unsure. Edmond and his family are Lebanese and don't have the option to evacuate, but we are glad they are with us and safe for now.

Praise God for this important answer to prayer, and continue to pray for our next steps toward leaving the country.

Salaam,

Nate

PARENTS WITH PASSPORTS

I had prepared a list of possible activities my parents and I could do while they were in Lebanon, and asked them to put a check next to the things that interested them. Mom was the more adventurous of the two. A year after marrying Dad she had quit teaching to stay home and raise her sons on his small salary as a sixth grade teacher. She had always wanted to travel more, so she enjoyed negotiating our itinerary by email in the months before their arrival in September. I think my dad would have been happier to stay at home, but he was a good sport and went along for Mom's sake. They had never left the United States and had to get passports for the first time.

I was excited for them to come, almost four months after my tour of the liberated South with Sadiq and Mustafa. Sharing my new life with someone from home would make it real. Back in the States, they would confirm my fantastical email reports to others. As the time for their visit drew closer, though, I got nervous. I wondered, as in countless times in the past, what their attitude would be and how I would react.

I remembered the day I graduated from college. My folks didn't leave Vashon Island very often, but they *did* come over to the mainland to attend my commencement ceremony. Afterward, they invited me out to dinner. I was so pleased to have them there, but the simple "congratulations" they extended left me unsatisfied. I felt guilty for wishing I could have spent those hours celebrating with my friends instead of with my parents.

My parents were stoics. They carefully measured their displays of emotion. Words of encouragement were an anomaly when I was growing up. On the other hand, I was careless and lazy then, and I disappointed them with bad choices. By the time I got my act together, they had settled into safe indifference and low expectations. After all, it had taken me way too long to complete college, and what was I going to do with a biblical studies degree anyway?

Now they were coming to the other side of the world to see what I had done with myself. *Maybe this time will be different.*

We planned too many activities for the length of their stay. We'd optimistically overlooked some limiting factors. Lebanon is hotter and more humid than Seattle. My parents were in their sixties and Mom was out of shape. It was the best vacation ever, but it wiped us all out.

In a two-day, overnight blitz of a drive, we covered half the main highways of the country. We toured the palace at Beit Eddine, the Baruk cedar grove, the wadi of Zahle, and the ruins of Baalbek in the Bekaa Valley.

The cedars fascinated Mom. To reach the Bekaa Valley, we scaled the Lebanon mountain range. The cedars were near the summit, before cresting and descending into wine and hashish growing country. The high elevation cooled down our hike through the remaining acres of the famous trees. My folks pushed themselves to the end of the trail where the largest tree spread out its impressive girth. No tree in the biblical world could compare with the cedar. King David's palace and the Temple of Solomon were built from them. They were synonymous with pride and glory. I could see Mom and Dad were humbled by the weight of history as I often was in Tyre. We rested in the shade and took in the breathtaking view of the coast below. Mom's feet were swollen.

On the way back, she started to stumble. Dad held her hand and steadied her. She struggled over roots in the path, and leaned on his seasoned farmhand strength for support. It was slow going, but she eventually made it back to the car.

Thirty years earlier, I had been the one complicating a hike on Mount Rainier. Paradise. That's where the lodge was and where the trail started. We wanted to go about the same distance of three miles, but to my little six-year-old legs the miles felt more like twenty. My parents were disappointed to turn back before reaching the ice caves they'd driven hours to see.

Roles were somehow reversing themselves. I should have foreseen Mom's limitations and taken them into account.

***

Sadiq was eager to welcome my folks and share with me the burdens and joys of providing hospitality. Honored guests of mine were honored guests of his as well. We had become brothers. One evening, we all gathered for dinner on the beach.

The public beach was just south of the Rest House Resort, within walking distance of Tyre. The mile-long stretch of sticky golden sand framed the sunset perfectly as colors shifted in the west over the Mediterranean. Each spring the municipality erected eighty restaurant huts in a long row above the high tide line as soon as it was collectively agreed upon that the sea was warm enough for swimming. Local restaurants staffed each hut with part-time cooks and offered a selection from the restaurant's regular menu. Diners sat on the beach side of the structures, where a mass of plastic tables and chairs provided relief from the evening heat of the concrete buildings in which everyone lived.

The four of us sat at a table in front of the place hosted by the Tyros restaurant. A few other early birds had arrived before us and were lounging with Pepsis and bowls of nuts or puffing on hookah pipes. Sadiq and I put our backs to the sea so Mom and Dad could watch the sunset. We chatted over the lull of the gentle waves.

"What do you think of Lebanon?" Sadiq asked.

Mom burst out, "It's been incredible!"

"If you like it, take it. It's yours!"

Sadiq's generosity was authentic. He won over my mom by listening with a warm smile as she gave her initial assessment and told stories of our adventures. Dad appeared to be enjoying the relaxed evening as he quietly watched and listened.

A gap in the conversation gave Mom a chance to take in the scenery. She pointed toward the lights of some buildings farther south down the beach. "Is that barbed wire on the beach between us and that town?"

Sadiq looked where she pointed over his shoulder, then turned back and explained, "That's *Rashidieh*. It's a camp for Palestinian refugees."

That caught Mom's attention, "So, it's like a prison?"

Sadiq and I looked at each other. I wondered how my parents would respond to this potentially inflammatory topic. I hoped she wouldn't offend Sadiq by saying something insensitive as he began to explain local politics.

"Palestinians are free to come and go, but they don't have the freedom of citizenship to buy and sell property or own businesses."

"Hmmm. Sounds like Native Americans on reservations in the United States," she said.

"Exactly!" Sadiq seemed pleased that my parents were interested. He was used to a world that had grown tired of hearing about Middle Eastern struggles. His eyes were fiery as he told how history had played out.

In 1947, the UN created a resolution to partition the land that they oversaw in their Palestinian Mandate after the Turkish Empire was destroyed. They agreed to form both a Jewish state and an Arab state in Palestine. Neither Jews nor Arabs were content with the land assigned to them, and the two groups went to war with each other in the wake of departing British troops in 1948.

Israel not only succeeded in holding off their Arab enemies, but also in taking land from both Egypt and Jordan along with all the territory that had been designated to make up the Palestinian state. Many of the displaced people fled to the neighboring countries of Lebanon, Syria, and Jordan. Over fifty years later they still found themselves as outcasts without a homeland.

Mom was aware of the Middle East peace process negotiations and she had heard of Israel's refusal to allow these refugees to return. She asked Sadiq why Lebanon couldn't just absorb these poor people into its population as citizens. It surprised me that Mom was interested in the politics. If I had thought about it, I might have grasped that the events Sadiq described had happened in Mom's childhood. He was filling in crucial pieces of the puzzle that Western media had neglected to report.

The Palestinian population was and is still a hot issue in Lebanon because of the country's confessional system of government. The parliament has always been elected according to religious affiliation. Citizens vote on different lists depending on which of the four major sects they belong to: Christian, Sunni Muslim, Shia Muslim, or Druze. The person whose name appears first on the Sunni Muslim list forms the parliament and becomes Prime Minister. The number of seats are awarded according to the religious demographics at the time, but the presidency is reserved for the top name on the winning Christian list. The premium political seat for Shia is Speaker of Parliament, and the best Druze post is Minister of Defense.

Surrounded by the dictatorships and kingdoms of the Muslim world, Lebanon clings to democracy, but the confessional system of government is problematic.

First, it creates internal strife *within* religious blocks, as each sect has only one designated powerful position to attain. Christian families divide tribally into mafia-like clusters, each with their own militias, working their way toward overpowering the other Christian families. Sunnis and Shia have their own internal battles and Druze to a lesser extent.

The waiter came with two bowls of mixed nuts and poured water. Mom mentioned she had never realized that Christians had fought against Christians and Muslims against Muslims. When the waiter asked to take our order, I told him we would have the specialty, *fatayl*, which was described in English on the menu as chicken *prepared in the Chinese way*. Then Sadiq eagerly returned to explaining how the confessional system tied in with the Palestinian problem.

Muslims had more children than Christians. Shia Muslims had more children than Sunni Muslims. Many Christians exercised their greater economic freedom and emigrated to other countries.

The state of Lebanon hadn't existed long before the Christian population shrank from most numerous to third most numerous – switching places with the Shia, who moved from third to first. The

Sunnis proved to be the balancing agent because they preferred being second to the Christians over being second to the Shia. The Sunnis formed a cooperative block with the Christians to preserve the status quo by ignoring the change in population. Lebanon has not had an official census since 1932.

The surge of Palestinians in the country after 1948 threatened the Christian-Sunni coalition because most Palestinians were Sunni Muslims. If they were granted citizenship, it would offset the demographic balance again and tempt the Sunnis to claim the right to replace Christian leadership themselves. Ironically, it is the animosity between Sunnis and Shia that ensures Christian governmental control in Beirut.

Both Mom and Dad were fascinated, nodding as Sadiq connected the dots for them. They wondered how things had gotten so complex in the first place. Sadiq was on a roll now. He continued passionately, plunging further back in time to the creation of Lebanon.

During World War I, the Ottoman Turks ruled the entire Middle East. The Turks fought with Germany against France and Britain. At that time, even before victory was remotely assured, France and Britain argued about how the Turkish Empire would be divided between them following the war, assuming that they won. Their arguments froze their cooperation and threatened their ability to succeed.

The conflict between the allies was solved by civil servants from each country. Sir Mark Sykes from England, and Charles Georges-Picot from France drafted a document dividing the Turkish Empire into geographic sections that would later become colonies for Britain and France. This document, known as The Sykes-Picot Agreement, set the borders for what would become Lebanon, Syria, Iraq, Jordan, and Palestine. Lebanon and Syria were assigned to France. Iraq, Palestine, and Jordan were to be retained by England. Lines were drawn quickly on a map with little regard to linguistic, ethnic, or cultural boundaries. The secret agreement was known only to Western powers and was undisclosed to the people of the lands under discussion. Britain and France agreed to the document and got on with winning the war, though they had no idea of the worldwide problems their presumptuous agreement would cause.

True to the Sykes-Picot Agreement, France was awarded a

mandate over Greater Syria after the war. The Catholic Maronite Christians along the coast were relieved at the prospect of their own protected nation in the midst of all their Muslim neighbors. New boundary lines were drawn to encircle a majority Christian region and in 1920, Lebanon was born as a French protectorate. It was the French who designed the confessional system in an attempt to preserve Lebanon's Western Christian flavor before granting it independence in 1943, but Beirut's golden days of fame as the *Paris of the Middle East* were numbered.

My parents listened intently, as if watching an action flick. They'd been charmed out of their usual composure. Our food arrived, and Sadiq sheepishly became conscious he'd been monopolizing the conversation. We ate in thoughtful silence until Mom looked Sadiq soberly in the eyes, "Thank you for helping me to finally understand it all." A lifetime of misunderstanding and Arab mistrust were erased in my parents' effort to travel the distance and meet a real person face to face, who had lived out the events.

***

One of the other options Mom had checked on the list was a tour along the southern border with Israel. The prospect of driving that road had an exciting and dangerous allure. She wanted the rush of standing on the border of the holy land. As we made our preparations we encountered an obstacle: there had been tension at the border, and travel to the South was more restricted than when Sadiq, Mustafa, and I had gone. The Lebanese Army now required foreigners to get permission to travel past key checkpoints into the formerly occupied zone. We would all have to go and accomplish this together at the army base 25 miles north of Tyre in the city of Sidon.

We got an early start and arrived in Sidon about 9:00 AM. I had been to the army base before with Denis, so I knew the way to get there.

At the first big traffic circle, I peeled off to the east. Defensive installations confirmed that I had chosen the right road. The road was wide enough to be considered a freeway, but concrete blocks covered in razor wire were placed on alternating sides of the road to require a lot of weaving at low speed. I parked at the barricade a couple blocks from our destination, and we got out of the car to walk the rest of the way to the gate.

Giant traffic-stoppers in the road were made by welding three sections of steel I-beam into four foot tall metal car wreckers that looked like the old-fashioned jacks that children played with in the 1950s. They were painted in red and white stripes so you couldn't miss them. My folks raised their eyebrows in silent respect and growing apprehension. We had a lot planned for the rest of the day and I moved quickly to put this errand behind us. The sun cooked the smell of dust up from the ground. A small guard shack stood next to the road barricade at the entrance.

"We would like to ask permission to visit the South," I said in the most careful Arabic I could produce. From previous experience I knew better than to try English. I had learned that few army officials knew English, and it frustrated them to have this shortcoming pointed out. They were irritated enough by my weak Arabic comprehension.

The guard responded with a quizzical look. A person needs patience and empathy to negotiate meaning with an adult who seems to have the intellect of a third grader and the dialect of a Martian. Fortunately, a nearby soldier caught what I meant. We were soon on our way across the compound with a chaperone, heading toward an officer who had the authority to grant our request. We passed luscious fig trees that seemed to create a breeze beneath them, making the base already cooler than the street.

Our destination was an office with the familiar atmosphere of bureaucratic activity. High ceilings, beige painted concrete walls, and curlicue Ottoman designs in the floor tiles suggested cultured authority. Facing the door from the farthest corner of the room, was a metal desk. A framed photo of President Emile Lahoud hung on the wall behind it.

My parents were seated on a low couch along the wall opposite the desk. The guns, uniforms, and military scowls had already taken a noticeable toll on their carefree morning. They played nervously with their passports. The low seating elevated their knees and made them look comically meek as they drank in their surroundings with wide eyes.

I was shown to the "hot seat" across the desk from the base

commander. As I began to explain our mission, a glass of tea was placed on the desk in front of me.

It became clear that the policy on allowing foreigners near the border had become stricter than I'd expected, but all that was at stake was an optional day trip. In regular visa renewal trips to the General Security office in Tyre, I was usually much more tense, as they had the power to revoke my permission to stay in the country. At the moment, the consequences of denial wouldn't adversely affect my life much, so I just kept trying. I continued in Arabic and negotiated meaning for the words I didn't know. My parents couldn't understand a word. Body language was all they had by which to gauge progress.

"*Why* do you want to go to the South?"

The officer apparently didn't get a request like this every day. His eyebrows furrowed with intensity as he spoke. The concern wasn't that we were spies, but for our safety. The Lebanese government didn't want to be embarrassed by Americans wandering into a mine field and getting themselves killed in a high profile way. He motioned for his uniformed assistant to collect our passports.

I continued our case while he flipped pages. "I've been living in Tyre for almost a year, and my parents have come to visit me from America. We have been touring the country, and I want to take them around the South tomorrow." I hoped that his sense of hospitality would prevail over his concerns.

He asked, "Do you have the phone number of someone in Tyre who will vouch for you?"

"Yes. You could talk to Mustafa."

I got permission to reclaim my phone from the front desk where I'd been asked to leave it. I called my friend, gave him a short explanation, and handed the phone to the official. Mustafa was a good character reference.

"Okay, you're welcome to go," he said waving his hand as if he were standing at the checkpoint himself. "But stay on the main roads."

That seemed like the end, but I wasn't convinced it would be that easy.

"Will I need a written note to show at the checkpoint?"

Now he was getting irritated. "No. If you go tomorrow like you said, then they will be expecting to see you." We quickly thanked him and left.

As we were walking back to the car, my dad said, "Wow, son, that was an amazingly tense situation and I'm proud of the way you handled it so confidently. You've certainly accomplished something in the year you've been here."

At least that was what I wished he would have said. In reality, my parents were both quiet during the rest of the drive to Beirut, recovering their composure. It would have been groundbreaking if one of them had been able to verbalize their pride to me, but that was too much for me to expect of them. *There had been that moment in the office.* I had seen the look of pride on their faces. For a moment, they were helpless and I controlled our destinies. Their low expectations had been exceeded. I had earned their respect.

The only thing Dad had checked on the list of options was to go bowling in Beirut, so he could brag to his bowling buddies back home. That was where we headed that afternoon. Bowling and vegetable gardening were Dad's sports since graduating from college football. He'd taught me how to bowl when I was a kid. Together, we joined Saturday morning father-son leagues. We even took home a trophy once.

We used the house balls at the four-lane bowling alley I found in the city. The ceiling was so low it made us claustrophobic. We had to be careful not to hop on the approach or we'd bump our heads. We bowled three lines of record breaking low scores, but we didn't care. It was experiencing this common bond again in an exotic place that made it special.

My parents left Lebanon exhausted after two weeks of near constant movement. It *had* been different this time. I was encouraged with a new sense of standing with them, for which I would soon be even more grateful. None of us knew then that Dad had already begun the internal battle with cancer that would take him from us five years later. My mom would face the anxiety of receiving my evacuation emails alone.

From: Nate Scholz
Sent: Tuesday, July 18, 2006
Subject: Day 7 — Morning

Dear Family and Friends,

Wow. It's amazing what a good night's sleep in a safe place will do for you when you haven't had it in awhile!

Now we wait for news from the embassy about evacuation. Through the help of many stateside assistants, I have been assured that we are registered and that someone has been assigned to handle our case. This is important news for us since we were unsure if they knew of our existence. We have still received no direct word from our government at all. This contributed to our desire to travel yesterday, thinking that we were more on our own than we actually were. Regardless, it is much easier for them to take care of us from here than it would have been from Tyre.

The rumored plan that seems to be forming is that we will be ferried from Lebanon to Cyprus, perhaps out of the port of Jounieh. Then, it will be up to us to arrange for travel from there to the States. We don't know how long this process will take or how difficult it might be, but we feel sure that the hardest part of the journey is now behind us.

Kimarie wanted me to brief you on our current habitation and the kids. The children were wonderful in the car yesterday. They slept and watched the scenery and played quietly with each other. This was truly a godsend. I can't imagine what the trip would have been like if they had been melting down. They were wild last night when we arrived after being cooped up for so long, but are nearly back to normal now – happy, busy kids.

We are staying in a small suite with hot running water and all the electricity we can use. We awoke to the peaceful sound of birds chirping outside our window. I am almost trembling with gratitude to God for what he has delivered us from. For several nights, as I went to bed, I considered the reality that we could be killed instantly in the night. As we set out on our drive yesterday, I knew that we might not all survive the trip. I made contingency plans in my mind of what to do if Denis's car was bombed ahead of us.

Not having a TV at our house meant that we didn't see much of what was going on in the country; we heard about it from friends. Last night, I watched some horrific scenes on local Lebanese television. I can't even bear to describe them to you. We hope that you will continue to pray for us, but please pray also for the innocent families who are perishing both physically and eternally in these days.

I feel like the mourning prophet, Jeremiah. "Terror on every side!"

If you have kids, give them a hug right now and tell them how much you love them.

Salaam,

Nate

ETERNAL QUESTIONS

On a lazy Saturday, I sat sipping tea with Mustafa. Business was slow, so he put his employees to work refurbishing the latest shipment of used air conditioner units. They set up a work station just outside the open shop doors on the sidewalk, scrubbing with various brushes and scouring pads on the dingy metal. The strong chemicals they used restored the whiteness of the appliances more than I would have thought possible.

No customers prevented us from our serious talk. "Mustafa, what do you think will happen to you after you die? Will you go to heaven?" I asked.

"We believe each of us has an angel next to each shoulder, watching everything we do. The angel on the right records all of our good works. The one on the left writes down every evil deed. On the Day of Judgment, all of the books the angels write will be placed on the scales. I hope that on that day my good deeds will outweigh the evil ones."

"So, if your life is judged to be 51% good, then you'll go to heaven?"

"No one can know in advance," he said. "Even if the scale tips in my favor, God is sovereign. We try to do the best we can, but he is free to decide as he wishes. We pray for his mercy and compassion."

I believed the situation was much more bleak. I said, "It's harder than you think to enter paradise."

Mustafa cocked his head, intrigued. "What do you mean?"

"Imagine that I'm holding a glass of ice cold water," I said. "I'm going to offer it to you to drink, but you should know that it has one small drop of urine in it." I held my empty tea glass out to him. "Here you go. Will you drink it?"

Mustafa wrinkled his nose in disgust, "Of course not!"

"But why not?" I argued, "It's 99.9% pure water."

He put his hand up and turned his head.

"Do you think it has too much urine? Okay, I'll pour half the glass out and fill it back up to the top with more pure water." I poured from an invisible pitcher. "There. Now it is 99.99999% pure. Now will you drink it?"

"No way," he was offended now.

I went on, "If you won't drink the water because of a tiny bit of filth, then what makes you think that God would accept you with 49% sin? God himself is 100% pure and he won't allow anyone near him unless he is also 100% pure. If you have ever committed the smallest sin, God will reject you like you rejected my imaginary glass of water. No matter what you do to add good deeds, you can't become totally purified again. It's impossible."

Mustafa was thinking deeply now. We sat quietly for a minute, the sound of scrubbing in the background.

I began again with a new thought. "It's a big problem, but maybe you're like me and you have this desire to be with God, and you know in your heart that God wants to be with you. Is that true?"

He nodded soberly.

"If God wants the relationship with us, but he knows that we can't do anything to purify ourselves, then he must already know another way we can be purified. How do you think he would go about making us as spotless as he is himself?"

I wanted to describe Jesus as the ultimate solution to the human sin dilemma, but my Muslim friends had preconceived ideas of who Jesus was and who he wasn't. They rehearsed arguments against foreign ideas until they popped out automatically when key words or phrases were introduced in conversation.

In Jesus' life, controversy surrounded him like a cloud obscuring him from clear sight. The answer to the question: *"Who is Jesus?"* was debated in Tyre and throughout the world, wherever his story was told.

Three hundred years after Jesus' earthly ministry, his followers were still trying to grasp the mechanics of his nature. The city of Tyre hosted a council of bishops to debate the different interpretations of Jesus' character. Their meetings led to the drafting of the Nicene Creed as an attempt to sort heresy from orthodoxy. Was Jesus in fact God, pretending to be man? Was Jesus a normal man whom God entered and possessed? Did Jesus have some secret power or knowledge that made him equal with God? Maybe Jesus was just another important prophet through whom God had spoken.

Reconsidering good ways to describe Jesus to Muslims challenged my own shallow understanding of him.

***

A traveling arts and crafts exhibit, called a *mawrad,* came to Tyre and was displayed under red and white striped canvas awnings erected in a vacant lot. Sadiq and I wandered in one evening to see what they were selling. Hand-made soap. Marble chess sets. Lacey tissue box covers. Paintings. A bright green splash of color arrested my attention and I walked closer to examine a framed work of art.

The figure in the painting hovered over the earth, which was in the background below. Rays of light shot away from his head. He wore the turban and black robe of religious leadership, but no arms or hands were visible. The artist had left me to assume the hands held the robe closed inside, like many men do, to keep from tripping over the edges while walking. The face was blanked out in a white shield, indicating that it depicted someone too holy to risk misrepresenting.

"Who do you think this is in the picture?" I asked Sadiq. I thought it might have been a Muslim perspective of Jesus.

"I'm not sure. Maybe it's the *Mahdi.*"

"The Mahdi? Who is that?"

"He is a future prophet who will appear on the Day of Judgment. We know Jesus will return to earth on that day, too. Some of my friends think that Jesus and the Mahdi are the same person."

The artist looked up, and Sadiq called her over to talk with us. "Who is the holy man in this painting? Is it the Mahdi?"

She glanced back and forth between us and went into strategic selling mode. She probably thought to herself, *If I say, "Jesus," the Westerner will be interested. If I say, "The Mahdi," then the Arab guy might buy it.* Instead of answering directly, she cagily evaded the question with another question, "Who do *you* think it is?"

I pressed her. "You must have had someone in mind when you painted it. Is it Jesus?"

She wouldn't name the character, but finally settled on her description and said, "It's the holy one who will come and rule the world and bring peace on the final day."

Sadiq helped me negotiate a price, and I bought the painting. I felt funny walking home along the beach with a large painting tucked under my arm. Sadiq wanted to keep talking about coming prophets. Our relationship had grown strong enough for him to confront what I believed, but from a position of respect, not disdain.

"We both agree that Jesus will arrive on the Day of Judgment, but we believe such different things about him. For example, how can you believe Jesus is the *Son of God*? The Koran teaches the truth, that Jesus was placed in Mary from the breath of God, not through their physical relations."

"Oh Sadiq, we believe the same thing about that. It's a big misunderstanding about what Son of God means. I know that the words "Son of…" are confusing, but it doesn't mean that Jesus is some kind of half god, half man like in Greek mythology or something. Actually, you believe that Jesus is the Son of God the same way I do."

"What? Impossible!" A boy looked up at Sadiq's outburst, and then went back to the sandy hole he was digging.

"Do you believe Jesus is *al-Masih*?" In Arabic, the word for *Messiah* is pronounced *MseeH* with a hard exhaled *H* at the end. In the biblical Greek, the same word is translated as *Christos*, or Christ.

"Of course. It's a name for Jesus in the Koran."

"What does the word mean? Do you know?"

Sadiq realized that he hadn't thought about that before. "No. I don't know." He had referred to Jesus his whole life as *Isa al-Masih*, just as many Christians treat *Christ* as Jesus' last name.

"It means *anointed*," I said.

"What's that?"

"It's when someone pours olive oil over your head."

"What? Why would they do that?"

"God told the Prophet Samuel to anoint David as a sign that he was chosen to be God's representative to his people. He was to be the designated ruler. After King David was anointed they referred to him by a new title – Son of God. It didn't mean that he was God, but that he *was* God's chosen man."

"What does King David have to do with Jesus?"

"After King David was a long line of bad kings. To give his people hope, God promised to someday send a greater king, who would be God's final appointed ruler over all humanity, not just the nation of Israel. Jesus is the one who is anointed as God's eternal choice, the master of creation. *Masih* and *Son of God* mean the same thing."

Sadiq replied, "Every prophet has something special about him, but we believe that they are all equal in importance." I had triggered the response of a default argument by suggesting that Jesus had a unique purpose and we returned to the shallow surface of known debating territory. As a resolution-seeking Westerner, I was still not accustomed to the non-linear thought processes of the Middle East.

We reached the landing on the stairs outside my door. I leaned the painting against the wall to get the keys out of my pocket. The white eyeless face stared at us a moment as I opened the door. I led the way to the kitchen and put the teakettle on the stove and turned on the burner. I rummaged through the cupboards for glasses, tea bags, and sugar.

Sadiq sat down at the kitchen table. "I also can't accept what you say about Jesus being hung on the cross to die. The Koran says, 'The Jews thought they had killed him,' but they were wrong. We believe that Jesus escaped crucifixion at the last minute. Instead, God made Judas Iscariot appear like Jesus, and the traitor was put on the cross in Jesus' place."

"I've been thinking about that sura from the Koran," I said. "I read something in the Bible the other day that explained it differently. Here, let's look at it. Just a second." I fetched my Bible from the bedroom and turned to the passage in the book of John.

The reason my father loves me is that I lay down my life –
only to take it up again. No one takes it from me, but I lay it
down of my own accord. I have authority to take it up again.
This command I received from my father. (John 10:17, 18)

I laid the Bible on the table. "So if Jesus was in control and voluntarily laid down his own life, then it makes sense that the Koran says the Jews only *thought* they killed him. Sheikhs teach that this sura in the Koran proves that Jesus didn't die, but could it be that it has been misunderstood? It doesn't literally say Jesus didn't die. It only says that the Jews didn't kill him."

The water boiled in the kettle. We continued to talk as I poured. The figure in the painting hovered before us on the counter where I'd propped it against the side of the refrigerator. Faceless. Armless. This painting portrayed the Muslim perspective of Jesus perfectly. They hadn't seen him in their mind's eye smiling at them. They hadn't imagined his arms around their shoulders.

I could almost hear him whisper to me, "...and who do *you* say that I am?"

From:	Nate Scholz
Sent:	Tuesday, July 18, 2006
Subject:	Day 7 — Evening

Hello Again,

Still waiting for word of an evacuation. Sounds like it will happen tomorrow or the next day, but nothing conclusive.

I spent the day servicing our car. We also had to find a municipality office to complete certain forms that will allow Edmond to sell our car for us. His car was probably destroyed in Tyre in the blast close to the hospital, so he may be driving the car instead. Kimarie spent most of the day with the kids and washed clothes. We both had a chance to go on a peaceful walk around the monastery grounds in the evening before dinner.

We have been eating three delicious meals a day in a comfortable dining hall, with caring sisters going to great lengths to fulfill our many needs.

I also took about an hour to call friends in Tyre to find out if they were okay. So far, everyone I know has either escaped to the mountains or is currently safe. There are miraculous stories of Druze and Christians in the hills taking Shia Muslim refugees into their homes.

We love you all and hope to see you again very soon.

Salaam,

Nate

Against All Odds

There's a subtle difference between liking solitude and embracing loneliness. I was 33 years old, a third of a century, when I followed Jesus to Lebanon. It seemed inevitable that the call to a life of chastity was part of the deal. If I had not found anyone to marry in my own culture with fifteen years of adult time to search, how could I expect to find someone I matched up well with in Lebanon? What were the odds? It would take a true miracle. Instead of getting too uptight about it, I asked God to somehow help me be content if I never got married. I wasn't there yet.

I expected a Hollywood experience. It's all incredibly clean in the movies. Love at first sight. The man finds the supermodel woman he deserves, and judging by the look of their apartment, she loves to cook and clean. Every woman gets a sensitive guy who's attentive to her feelings and keeps his body tan and muscular. I had unrealistic expectations of finding someone with all the qualities I was looking for, but I neglected the qualities in myself that a prospective wife might want. What if God was preparing someone for me? This faceless woman would deserve a man who had preserved his purity for her. She would want a courageous, confident man, who would lead in the relationship and guard her heart and provide for her. At the very least, she would want me to get rid of the spare tire I was carrying around from eating too much Arabic bread. I couldn't control whether or not someone fell in love with me, but I resolved to develop loveable attributes in myself. I could meet my soul mate tomorrow or it could be twenty years away.

In the mean time I grappled with the amazing concept that I could be satisfied in God alone. I envisioned myself overcoming my discontentment by practicing the presence of God like the monks in history who had gone about their daily business in constant prayer and meditation. Had they succeeded? Had God provided for *all* their needs through Christ Jesus? I was sure they were at least better off than me. I asked God to show me how to be the husband my future wife deserved and to satisfy all my needs for companionship in himself until I met her, however long that might be.

***

My friend Sadiq underwent the same struggle. Cultural differences didn't negate the core human longing for intimacy.

"Tell me about arranged marriages, Sadiq. Will the couple be meeting each other for the first time today?" A light breeze flitted through the valley on a July evening. Sadiq had invited me to a wedding at The Palace in the countryside just south of Tyre.

"Of course not," he laughed. "You're not in *India*."

It was almost 6:30, and we had arrived late because of me. When I stopped to pick him up, Sadiq was horrified that I wasn't wearing a tie. We took the time to return to my apartment so I could formalize myself appropriately. Now we sat at one of fifty tables in an outdoor banquet area. Only a few dozen of the other guests had arrived before us. The tablecloth was topped with a bottle of water and bowls of mixed nuts. We settled in and took in our surroundings.

The Palace was especially designed for weddings – a lucrative business from the looks of it. The tables were spread out in a semi-circle around a dance floor shadowed by intensive rigging for laser lights and disco balls. Beyond the dance floor was the royal dais with his and hers thrones for the newlyweds to survey their subjects.

Sadiq continued, "When a guy decides to get married, he starts to look around for a prospective bride. If he finds someone he likes, he asks a member of his family to go and meet with her parents to suggest the arrangement. If her parents think the match is good then they talk it over with their daughter."

"So the girl has a choice?"

"Sure. She can say no if she wants to."

"Does she get to meet him before she decides?"

"Well, Tyre is small enough that most of the time they already know of each other, but they can also spend time together. There's usually a cousin or aunt who keeps an eye on them. After a while, they make a decision to get married or not." Sadiq scanned the crowd for friends to greet. More guests had arrived, and the air buzzed with chatter. A dozen little girls wearing miniaturized bridal gowns danced to soft music on the dance floor. A waiter hustled to replace the empty nut bowls.

"So what will we see here tonight?" I asked. "Is there a religious ceremony with vows?"

"No, no, no. This is the party. They *wrote the book* months ago. That's a private ceremony in the bride's family home. The families dress up and the sheikh comes and they sign papers."

"What?" My face wrinkled with confusion. "Months ago? Why did they wait so long?"

"Yes, it takes a lot of preparation to plan and finance the party and put a house in order. They've been legally married, but they continued to live separately until now." Dusk had overtaken the yellows in the sky, and most of the tables were crowded with guests. They were getting up and drifting toward the wide stairs at the entrance to the courtyard. Sadiq stood and pulled my arm, "C'mon. The bride and groom are arriving."

A troop of musicians in traditional Lebanese costumes, complete with ornamental scimitars, had joined most of the wedding party in the parking lot. Loud music started as a black Mercedes slowly approached with fresh white flower arrangements tied to the hood and door handles. Tambourines, hand drums, and nasal sounding flutes signaled the beginning of festivities as the couple emerged pristine from the car in black tuxedo and sequined white gown. They sauntered regally along the cobblestones, flanked by the gathered community. A parade of swirling dancers cocooned them as they strode, blending in motion with the musicians, swords flashing in the air.

As the couple and their entourage passed over the dance floor, the banks of colored spotlights and lasers responded with dazzling twirls. The celebrated king and queen completed the journey to their elevated thrones with cheers and applause. Noteworthy guests approached them to pay homage.

I asked more questions as we returned to our table. "She looks a lot younger than the groom. Is there some kind of rule about marrying younger women?"

"It's just the way it is," Sadiq lamented. "You have to get your life together before you can get married. No girl will agree to marry without a house and furniture, and maybe a car. Then there's the bridal set of gold jewelry, and the cost of the wedding. This party is probably costing $30,000. You know what the economy is like around here. There's no way regular guys like me can save up enough to get married before we're at least thirty, maybe forty. Only those from wealthy families can afford to get married young."

The waiters raced back and forth in full force, delivering bags of Arabic bread and plates covered with various Lebanese dishes in the mezze style. Every inch of real estate on the table in front of us was soon covered.

Sadiq went on between bites. "I liked a girl in high school, but I knew better to think that I could marry her. It wasn't long after we graduated that she was engaged to an older guy. You have to wait until you're prepared before starting to look, or you'll just get disappointed." He thought about it for another minute. "I'm sure the girls would rather marry someone their own age, but they can't just wait for years while the guy they like tries to succeed. When someone else asks about them, they'll take the guy who's ready for sure, if they get a guarantee that life will be comfortable for them."

I'd touched a bitter subject, and concentrated on the tasty food to offer Sadiq a break from my barrage of questions. After the meal, the music volume eliminated any ability to exchange information that you couldn't shout into an ear. When the *dabke* music started to play, Sadiq dragged me into the circle to show off the foreigner whom he'd trained in the national dance.

Around 11:00 PM the couple ceremonially approached a cake that was as tall as they were and together they cut it with a saber. More eating. More dancing and sweating. Ties and jackets came off. The grand finale of the evening came at 1:00 AM. The bride and groom made their way to the awaiting car while a parade of dancers and musicians swirled around them. As the door closed and the car pulled away, an impressive pyrotechnic show was executed to rival the nightly Disneyland fireworks. The crowd dispersed as others rushed to join the parade behind the wedding couple and zigzag through the streets honking their horns.

Sadiq and I retrieved our cameras and jackets. We had grown to be good friends, but the time we had to spend together was ending. An opportunity had opened up for Sadiq to work outside the country. He said, "Now that I've got that job in Saudi, I can start talking about getting married. I asked my mom and sisters to set up a meeting with a family before I go. I might be busy from now on as I prepare." I didn't know it then, but my own path had an upcoming turn.

***

Kimarie and I had met in England in August of 2000, just a month before my parents visited Tyre. I was escaping the heat of a Lebanese summer in London and attended a Dudley Woodberry lecture. I arrived early and chose a place to sit in the middle of the inclined lecture hall seating.

Then she came in.

She wore bib overalls over a short shirt that left her midriff exposed. She entered through the door at the right-front of the hall and crossed the room. Her long brown hair swayed at her waist and I noticed the gold pin in her nose as she passed by. She climbed the steps and took a seat a row behind me to the left side. I have no recollection of what Dr. Woodberry said that day. Instead of listening to him, I engaged in a mental civil war.

Don't look over there. It'll be too obvious. You're in front of her, she'll notice. Glance. Doh! I told you not to look! She caught you. I tried to concentrate on what was being taught. Perhaps I managed a couple minutes of restraint. *She might not have thought that you were checking her out that time, but if you look again, she'll know for sure.*

I know... but I... just... can't... help it. Stretch... Casual glance... Caught! *Dang! She might be looking at me now. Lean back, look nonchalant. Should I look to see if she's looking?* I was pathetically enslaved to the magnetic demands of my eyes on that alluring patch of bare skin and the exotic glint of gold in a nostril. *Man, what am I going to have to do to overcome this weakness?* I thought. *How can I pretend that I even want to be satisfied in God alone?*

Lunch was available after the lecture in the school's cafeteria. I was eating with a small group in the middle of a long row of tables. I saw Kimarie turn up the row with her orange plastic tray and we made eye contact again. She put her food down next to me and pulled out the chair to sit down. "Have we met somewhere before?" She asked. *Oh brother, that's a smooth pick up line.*

"I don't know. Where do you think it might have been?" I asked. "I'm from the Seattle area."

"I'm from Snohomish! *Where* in the Seattle area do you live?"

"Well, I live in Lebanon right now, but I grew up on Vashon Island."

"Lebanon? That's cool. I work for a trekking company in Kashmir, India." She said. "Where did you go to school? I went to Seattle Pacific University."

"I went to the Lutheran Bible Institute in Issaquah."

"Really? One of my best friends went there – Dawn Devlin."

"I know Dawn! She and her husband James are good friends of mine. All three of us were Residential Assistants together in the dorm."

Though we discovered mutual friends, we couldn't come up with a place we would have actually met. The conversation ended and we left to resume our individual travel plans without thinking to exchange contact information. Such a momentary connection surely couldn't lead anywhere, and I didn't think she was "my type" anyway, whatever *that* might mean.

A few weeks later, back in Lebanon after my parents had returned to the States, my destiny was changed by an email. It was from my college friend, James Aalgaard, who was married to Kimarie's friend Dawn. He had become a pastor to a small congregation in Oregon. His confirmation class students wanted overseas pen pals. He was writing to everyone he knew who lived abroad. As I replied to his message I noticed the other names of people he had included in the header of his email message. *Kimarie Ware? There can't be too many people named Kimarie in the world.* I harvested the address from the message and wrote to her and found that it was her.

Our first conversation centered on what we should say to James's group. It could have ended naturally right there, but messages ended with questions, and replies kept coming to answer them. "What is living in India like?" "How do Muslims observe Ashura in Lebanon?" Next came a list of standard questions. "What's your favorite ice cream flavor?" "If you were stranded on a deserted island and could have only one book aside from the Bible, what would it be?" Our messages progressed in length and frequency.

After six months my interest was more than casual, but I didn't have the courage to do more than hint about it. What followed was a finely crafted exchange in the not-quite-concealed junior high school game of "I wonder if she really likes me?" It began with an offhand suggestion that we should meet up in the Seattle area. We had both planned trips that would overlap. Carefully, we bantered back and forth about how we could negotiate our schedules. Neither of us wanted to be the first to risk exposing our interest, but it all came out as we made plans to travel together to James's church to make a combined presentation. The time spent in the car would be an opportunity to explore what a future together might look like. The term *courtship* was introduced to the discussion...

I offered to pick Kimarie up at the airport and drive her to her parents' house since I had arrived in the States ahead of her. On the appointed day and time, I waited at her gate, wondering if I would recognize her when she got off the plane. I hadn't seen any photos of her since our last meeting, so I was going on a year-old fleeting memory. She had emailed me that she'd be wearing a purple dress.

After finding one another, our conversation lurched and stumbled as we proceeded to baggage claim. Carefully constructed email messages had given me the ability to feel polished, but sizing each other up in person demanded instantaneous responses.

The awkwardness continued as we drove north from the airport. We stopped to eat dinner at a seafood restaurant on Lake Union and finally eased into comfortable recognition. We had gotten to know each other already. Writing had attracted us and given us a reliable footing on which to build. I could breathe a sigh of relief.

Then it was time to meet her parents.

Kimarie's uncles, aunts, cousins and parents lived on connected properties on a hillside above Mount Vernon. They called it Ware Mountain. Kevin and Kari Ware lived in an impressive country home. We turned up the long driveway and stopped at a wrought iron gate to enter the code into a keypad. The gate opened. I helped Kimarie carry in her suitcases and was invited in to chat for a few minutes.

Kimarie's parents no doubt wanted to catch up with their daughter who'd been in India for two years, but they had to deal with this strange guy whom they'd never heard of, as far as I knew.

We sat together in their living room. Kimarie gave the initial introductions. "We met in England. Nate lives in Lebanon and is back for a few months, *blah, blah, blah.*" My heart was pounding in my chest, and it was suddenly too hot and sweaty in there. "So what do you plan to do during your time in the States, Nate?" asked Dr. Ware. I tried to keep my cool. Here was my chance to ask, but how to do it smoothly? *Remember to make eye contact.*

I listed off a few things. A trip to Minnesota... A vacation with my family... Some speaking engagements... "And I was hoping to spend the time courting your daughter if I have your permission." There. I'd said it, right there in front of Kimarie and her mom, too – the courageous act of a lifetime.

It was Dr. Ware's turn to squirm in response to the unexpected and unusually blunt request. "Well, I don't know that you need to ask *me*," he sputtered, "but I think that her mother and I are okay with that." After another few minutes of chatting, I returned to my car for the triumphal drive home, with perma-grin on my face.

During the next couple of weeks, Kimarie and I created opportunities to do things with our friends and family: a camp with my church, a birthday party for her dad. She even went to a baseball game and suffered the humiliation of wearing a Mariners jersey. It didn't take long for me to come to my own conclusion. After a long talk on a hike together in the Olympic Mountains, I felt confident she was the woman I wanted to marry. She sensed that my own questions had been resolved, but discretely made me aware that she wouldn't yet entertain a proposal. It wasn't likely that I would have enough time to persuade her before I was due to return to Lebanon. I could put some hope on our upcoming trip to Oregon, but I had to be patient. In the meantime, I planned to visit friends in Minnesota.

Hi Gang,

Nothing new. Still waiting to receive word that we are to go get on a boat. I don't have as much to write about, so I am dropping back to an email a day.

Salaam,

Nate

I WAS IN
MINNEAPOLIS

My musician friend, Dan, flew with me to Minneapolis to visit my old college buddy. Bill and I had paired up as study partners in our torturous Greek class. The suffering we endured together cemented our friendship. Everyone liked Bill. He was generous with his skill of fixing cars. I think he could fix anything. He carved carousel horses out of laminated blocks of wood for a hobby. I was a groomsman when he and Gracia married.

We resumed our old friendship as if the ten-year gap since school didn't exist. Bill had become a junior high school shop teacher and he and Gracia had a handful of little kids. The first morning of our visit, we headed out to tour Bill's school building. Dan and I complained about being caffeine deprived.

"Sorry guys," Bill said on the way out the door. "We don't have any coffee in the house, but we'll stop on the way. I want to introduce you to my friend Yusef. He works at the gas station down the street and he speaks Arabic. You can get your coffee fix there."

"There're no guarantees that I'll be awake enough to speak Arabic if I haven't had the coffee ahead of time," I jabbed. "Where's he from?"

"I don't know. I never asked him."

Yusef stood at the counter and greeted Bill as we walked in the door of the quick mart. Bill introduced Dan and me. I went right into Arabic.

"Tsharafna, ya Yusef. Keifak? Inshallah mneh?"

The Arabic lit his face up with curiosity. I soon learned why.

We continued speaking in Arabic. He asked, "How did you learn Arabic?"

"I've been living in Lebanon for two years."

"Are you serious? *I'm* from Lebanon! Where were you living?"

"In Tyre," I said.

He said, *"I'm* from Tyre!" *Could this be happening? Was the world really this small?* He had recognized my southern Lebanese dialect the moment I started talking. "What part of the city?" he asked.

"Hay Ramel."

"No way! Seriously? What building?"

"Halawayni Center."

"My family lives just around the corner from you!"

We both reeled at the unlikelihood of the coincidence. We may have been the only two people in Minnesota who had lived both in the US and in Tyre. We felt at home with each other instantly in the way that shared experience can make you feel understood and known. I turned to Bill and Dan and translated what we'd discovered to them. They shook their heads in disbelief.

We took our drinks to go, but I already looked forward to the next several mornings of coffee conversations. Dan would fly back to Seattle the next day for work, but since I was staying, I could talk to my new Tyrian friend again.

The day I met Yusef was September 10, 2001.

I was still tired when Gracia woke Dan and me early the next morning. *Why is she getting us up anyway? We don't need to be anywhere.* I was annoyed.

She walked past our sleeping bags and turned on the TV. "Bill heard something big happened – a plane crash in New York." She said. We sat up and watched a waking nightmare. A commercial jet had crashed into one of the twin towers of the World Trade Center in New York City and reporters were trying to sort out what was going on. *Could it have been an accident?* Cameras trained on the smoke pouring out of the North Tower captured live footage of a second plane as it flew into the South Tower. We no longer doubted that a coordinated attack was underway.

My spine chilled. As events unfolded, it didn't seem they could possibly be real.

Smoke rose from a broken Pentagon building after a third plane barreled into it.

A fourth plane crashed to the ground in Pennsylvania after passengers disrupted the hijackers' plans to attack another unknown target. *The White House?*

The first tower to fall was the South Tower, even though it was the second to be hit. No one expected it to collapse. *Did the terrorists know that would happen?* The distant camera angle we were seeing on the news miniaturized the scene. I couldn't cope with acknowledging the death that I witnessed as the building melted downward in a cloud of dust. It was like watching a science fiction movie where toy boxes were used to create the effect of reality. *How many people were inside?*

It wasn't long before the North Tower fell too. In the space of two hours the World Trade Center went from *business as usual* to being erased.

The mayhem happened thousands of miles away in New York and Washington D.C., but it felt as if we would soon learn that the entire country was under attack at once. Suddenly, any danger seemed possible. The cement walls of Bill's basement around us were a comfort, giving me the feeling of being in an underground bunker. *Could they somehow get to us here? Now?* That scale of physical invasion was impossible in the United States, but psychological ground was taken that day in every American heart.

The news reports identified the attackers as Muslim extremists. They had synchronized the hijacking of commercial flights, turned them into human-bearing missiles, and flown them into their other targets. It was the highest profile terrorist act in history, taped and replayed to satellite dishes everywhere.

The international community looked on with us and knew that the world would never be the same again. One of the key Bible passages I studied about Tyre came to mind: a prophetic message predicting the fall of the seemingly impregnable city.

"Now the coastlands tremble on the day of your fall; the islands in the sea are terrified at your collapse." (Ezekiel 26:18)

Who would have thought that the United States was so vulnerable?

Air traffic was grounded nationally, and Dan couldn't go home that day. We didn't even try to go to the airport. If I would have been told a week earlier that every plane in United States airspace would be grounded, I would have laughed at the absurdity of the suggestion.

There was still no coffee in the house. About mid-afternoon, Dan and I ventured out to the gas station to check on Yusef. The place was more crowded this time. Customers were eating in the snack area, talking in hushed tones. The mourning process had already begun, and people were progressing from denial into anger. That's why it was particularly unfortunate that I chose to greet Yusef in Arabic.

"As-salaamu Aleikum," I said.

The sense of connection we shared the day before vanished instantly. I had unthinkingly just called attention to everyone within earshot that he was an Arab. I might as well have painted a bull's-eye on him. He mumbled a hello in English, and made himself busy behind the counter. We didn't have so much common experience after all. Yusef was better acquainted with fear than I was and knew the art of discretion and caution. He was right to be fearful. Mosques across the country would be vandalized in the following days.

Footage of celebrations in Muslim areas of the world inflamed thoughts of revenge and suspicion. Angry Americans went out and acted on those feelings, hate for hate. The problem was that they didn't know who the Muslims were. Punjabi Sikhs were pulled from taxicabs and beaten, just because they wore turbans.

Americans reacted in different ways. Some projected a bloodthirsty, subhuman nature on all Muslims and responded by nurturing their own fears and hatred. Others wondered what kind of injustice could motivate such desperate acts and began to probe for answers.

I later learned from a news article what motivated one of the ringleaders, Mohammed Atta. In 1996 he had watched breaking video footage of the massacre in Qana, Lebanon in his dorm room in Germany. Maybe he saw the same unfading image of the half baby that I did on New Year's Day in 2000. The effect on him was a desire for revenge at any cost. He picked up his pen that day, wrote his martyrdom will, and started figuring out how to fly a commercial jet into the New York World Trade Center.

I worried for Denis in Tyre. *Would our neighbors be celebrating there?* I got through to him that night.

"What's going on there? Are you okay?" I asked.

"We're okay," he said, "I had no idea what to expect as I got ready to leave our building this morning, but I needed to know how the community was reacting."

"Did you hear people celebrating?"

"No. I was overwhelmed by their concern for us. Every person in our neighborhood I talked with asked how we were feeling and dealing with the news. They asked if we had any relatives or friends who had been caught in the tragedy. You know some of them have relatives in the States and are just as concerned for them as we are for our own families. They all shared their shock and disbelief at such a strike against innocent people. They've experienced the same kind of loss through bombing and massacre over the last 25 years around here."

I was relieved that my hopes were realized. I couldn't imagine my friends thinking of this as a positive event.

He went on, "Our tailor friend said that he felt he was on the verge of a heart attack as he watched the news breaking. Another guy in the neighborhood said that there is no possible way that the people who did it could even be called human and yet do such an outrageous thing."

"So you guys feel safe?"

"Yes, but I'm thinking about Muslim families in the States right now being targeted for hate crimes. Please let people know that not all Muslims are happy about this attack."

Sadiq emailed from Saudi Arabia, where he had moved for work, and he copied the email to Denis as well. He wrote:

Dear brothers and friends, I was shocked when I heard about what happened in the US, and it reminds me of what happens all the time in the world in different sizes and shapes because there is no belief in justice and peace. I feel that the

End is coming because of all these crazy actions everywhere.

> *I pray to God that nothing happened to anyone related to you because I know how you are feeling. I have lived through these feelings in losing friends and relatives. I am very sorry and I wanted to share my feelings with you, my brothers. May God send his peace to the entire world.*

We tried to get Dan home on the twelfth. The airline phone numbers were inaccessible, so we drove to Minneapolis-St. Paul International Airport. We thought we'd just go talk to someone in person about rescheduling his flight. We circled the departures drive slowly. There wasn't a car or person in sight. The skies were unnaturally silent. It was like we'd stepped back in time a hundred years, or forward into some apocalypse. We didn't bother getting out of the car to check the doors.

It's hard to imagine now how differently we thought in America before September 11, 2001. We've undergone a fundamental shift toward a collective fear. Before, we felt invincible. Now, we are obsessed with security. We've proven that we're willing to give up a lot to try and feel invincible again.

Hello All,

We got up today and found that we still hadn't received an email or a phone call from the embassy. However, we heard that US Marines are prepared to take out 2,000 Americans from the coast today, and 4,000 tomorrow.

Again, we've made the decision not to sit still for too long. Denis will drive us down to the port in about an hour and we will attempt to be processed for departure today. Denis will remain for at least another day in order to make sure that Edmond's family is taken care of for housing. If we get turned back today we can call Denis and have him come back and pick us up to return to the monastery.

We have heard that we won't be required to pay for the boat trip to Cyprus, and also that the State Department may be chartering planes to take people directly to Washington DC and points beyond.

Cash is scarce right now. Banks are only allowing small amounts to be withdrawn at a time through ATM machines, and only in Lebanese pounds. We had hoped to leave a big chunk of money with Edmond, but it looks like we will have to use much of what we have left on hand for our lodging costs here at the monastery. They don't have the option of accepting a credit card payment, but they did agree to accept a personal check for two-thirds of the amount.

Kimarie is packing up our stuff again as I am writing and sending this message. It is a little after 9:30 AM now, and we will probably be at the port by around 11:00 AM. Please pray that we are successful in getting processed and onto a boat TODAY.

Salaam,

Nate

Surviving Storms Together

My conviction that Kimarie was the woman God had prepared for me brought a revelatory thought. "Dan, I need to buy a ring!"

We had gotten on a plane together and said goodbye to Bill in Minnesota. Now, as Dan and I got in the car to drive back to the island, my attention returned from hijackings and shifted to Kimarie. Dan knew I had no room for a diamond in my budget, and I needed his advice. Even a small chance that she would be won over meant that I should be ready. He didn't answer right away. I took my eyes off the road to glance at him.

"You don't need to spend another minute worrying about it, Nate," he said. "I think God's got you covered." He had that I-know-more-than-I'm-telling look on his face, as if he'd been praying about this long before I'd thought of it.

A week later, a gift arrived from someone who wished to remain anonymous. I opened two velvet boxes to discover his and hers diamond rings. The receipt was enclosed, along with instructions about which jewelry store to go to if I preferred to exchange the rings for something else. I took my mom shopping with me and she helped me pick out a round brilliant cut diamond in a solitaire setting that

I could have for the value of both the other rings plus the couple hundred dollars I had scraped together.

Two months after I'd met Kimarie at the airport, we drove together to meet with James Aalgaard's youth group in eastern Oregon. The many miles ticked by on the odometer, unnoticed. A key negotiation between sovereign nations was underway.

Kimarie was getting to the crux of her doubts: "You *seriously* haven't thought about any dreams for your future?" She had detailed a set of plans she had written in college that she was in the process of checking off as she accomplished them.

"I guess I was raised to take life a day at a time." I was thinking out loud, trying to figure it out myself. "I was happy to pay off my college debts and get to Lebanon. I planned to grow old there."

"If Lebanon is your dream, then where do *I* fit in?" She asked.

"What do you mean?"

"Are you mostly interested in me because I'm open to going there with you? What if you had to choose?

Good question.

"If push came to shove, would you give up your plans of returning to Lebanon in favor of me, or is being there more important to you?" There it was: the pregnant moment of decision.

As a single guy, I was free to prioritize what I saw as God's calling on my life, but God could lead me somewhere else at any time. Marriage was for life. It wasn't a question of *What if I had to choose?* I did have to choose. *Right then.* I had been waiting for the moment to get down on one knee, but this was the proposal that truly mattered to her.

I had made a decision like this before. Someone asked me once if I wanted to spend the rest of my life with Jesus. I raised my hand and gave up my own plans. *You call those plans?*

She waited patiently for my answer. You could have heard the sound of the last tumbler falling before the opening of the door to a safe.

"Whether we wind up going to Lebanon or not, we can create some new dreams together. I choose you, Kimarie."

She smiled. "As long as I'm confident that I come first in your life, Nate, I will follow you anywhere. Lebanon would be fine."

***

Planning a wedding is a lot of work, of course. We had the most fun arranging food for the reception. Kimarie found Mr. Mohammed, a Pakistani Muslim whose restaurant menu boasted a combination of East Indian and Lebanese cuisine. With him as our caterer, we represented the best food from each of our most recent homes. We asked him to prepare chai tea, naan bread, and chicken tikka masala along with kafta kabobs and hummus. Kimarie's mother and my mom each made delicious Norwegian and German desserts from our respective countries of ancestry.

Not long before the wedding, Kimarie was sharing our meal plans with a girlfriend who called to RSVP. "You're going to have a Muslim caterer?!" she asked in shock. "Are you sure that's a good idea? I mean, it would be the perfect terrorist opportunity to poison us all." We shouldn't have been as surprised as we were at her fears. Our perspectives had diverged from those of many of our Western friends as a result of experiences with Muslims.

Kimarie and I joked that we kept the travel industry alive after September 11 from all the guests who traveled long distances to come to our wedding. Several drove or flew from different states, but Kimarie's roommate Charlene came from Kashmir, and Denis came from Tyre to be in the wedding party. I was thirty-six years old, and many of my friends had long since given up hope that I would tie the knot. It must have seemed as miraculous to them as it did to me.

The day of the wedding came – April 20, 2002. It was held at University Presbyterian Church in Seattle. Our mutual friend, James Aalgaard, officiated our union. We reserved our first kiss for our wedding day, though few of the guests knew. We had decided to wait until Kimarie was wearing the ring God gave us. We didn't shoot off fireworks or hire dancers to wield swords, but there *were* about 300 guests.

No one was poisoned at the reception, though people left lots of leftovers. In hindsight, it was understandable that the kafta kabobs were left alone. If people weren't used to eating ethnic foods, it stood to reason their first choice wasn't going to be a long tube of brown meat that kind of resembled a turd.

We waited six months to move to Lebanon. Wise friends counseled us to integrate our lives and build our marriage relationship before attempting to add the stresses of living in another culture. We used the time to equip ourselves for the jobs we planned to do in Tyre. Kimarie took classes in Teaching English as a Foreign Language and I prepared to add computer classes to the offerings of the language center. We rented a one-bedroom apartment in the Norwegian neighborhood of Ballard in Seattle. By the time we arrived in Tyre, on Kimarie's twenty-ninth birthday, Sadiq had left to work in Saudi Arabia and he was still single. It felt strange living in Tyre again without my friend around. Kimarie and I were negotiating where the end of self and the beginning of spouse were located.

I had honored my Muslim friends for the previous two years by fasting during the month of Ramadan with them, in the same way that they did. They knew that I wasn't a Muslim, but it was an opportunity to gain the respect of neighbors as a man who took his faith seriously. When I was unmarried, living by myself, it was also a great way to get invited to home-cooked Iftar meals at sunset every night for the month. I learned more about my adopted culture than I could have lifting tea glasses in shops during the day.

The benefits of participating in the season seemed so obvious to me that I completely assumed Kimarie would be excited to join me in the discipline. She didn't want to, but she said she didn't mind if *I* did. Ramadan started a couple weeks after we arrived, giving us just enough time to find a new place to live and get a head start on furnishing it.

Our hunt for a living space had been fairly quick and easy, but the place we decided on needed some preparation before we could move in. Amazingly, the eleventh floor apartment had a one hundred and eighty degree view of the Mediterranean Sea, facing west for perfect sunsets. Even more amazing, was that the owner of the flat was the sister of Yusef, the guy I had met in the quick mart coffee shop in Minnesota. Their father handled the details of the rental agreement.

Now that I was married, the invitations for Iftar meals dried up. It would have been insulting to Kimarie for us to be asked, like suggesting that she wasn't capable of preparing meals for her husband. We did have a few nights of shared meals with our new neighbors across the hall, a Sunni family, Kamel and Amina and their four kids. Another couple from the seventh floor were close friends with Kamel and Amina and always over visiting at their apartment: Noor, a conservative Shia woman, and her Christian husband, Tony.

Most nights, Kimarie cooked for her famished husband to eat voraciously at sunset, though she got hungry and ate earlier herself. Not eating our meals together for a month shortly after our arrival created emotional distance. One night Kimarie broke down and sobbed after several trying days, "You care more about fasting than you do about me!"

With little sympathy I persisted to the end of the observance that year. I just didn't understand what the big deal was. I tried my best to negotiate my resolve with her desire for a sense of belonging, but I should have quit fasting as soon as I saw that it bothered her. It was the second time I'd screwed up communicating my faith through fasting. Disciplines that we adopt to express our devotion to God ought not to damage our relationships with our loved ones. My spiritual relationship with God should complement my love for people and vice versa.

On a stormy Saturday night in December, a few days after Ramadan was over, we came home from an evening of visiting. The sea across the street from our building tossed violently over the buffer of rocks onto the sidewalk and street. The palm trees swayed and gyrated with their fronds standing off to the landward side, madly grasping at the nearby building. The power to run the elevator was out, and we trudged up the dark stairs, guided by the dim light from my cell phone. The wind whistled through broken stairway windows and rain flew in laterally to create puddles on the marble landings. Phone cables that normally hung limp against the outside of the building thrashed back and forth, thwacking the walls with the force of a bullwhip.

We reached our floor and unlocked the heavy plate-metal outer door and swung it against the wall by the useless elevator. As I pulled open the inner wooden door, the change of air pressure inside the room caused the high winds to shatter the sliding glass deck door like a grenade. Shards of glass were blown down the hall to the other side of the apartment, three rooms away. It was after midnight already, but we had to work past our weariness to quickly rescue our new curtains and furniture from the invading storm. We shouted to hear each other over the screaming wind. As we rolled up the soaked carpets, we were drenched by the ice-cold rain ourselves. We worked in the dark, with only the moonlight that made it through the clouds. We took care not to cut ourselves on the broken glass. Some jagged edges still stuck to the aluminum frame, jutting out like broken teeth.

We were afraid that the windows on the other end of the house would also break from the pressure, so we opened them, which then made the hall a perfect wind tunnel. We could have rented it to Boeing to test the aerodynamics of their airplane wings.

Exhausted, we retreated to sleep on the floor in the corner of the office as the best location to offer protection from the tempest we had invited in. I set the alarm clock to wake me up every hour so I could squeegee the floods out of our living room. I got soaked over and over again as I waded in with my flip-flops and shoved the water over the aluminum threshold with the long handled rubber scraper that sometimes served to mop the floors. With each push, the wind would throw half of the water back against my legs. It took fifteen minutes to coax the gallons to the balcony drain. I'd dry off and take a nap with the alarm set for the next hour. Close to dawn, the rain finally relented.

Kimarie and I had faced our first stormy season together and survived.

Still here. What a mess.

We prayed together this morning as a group for what we thought was the last time. Tears and heavy hearts all around, mourning for our community of three families that was about to be separated. We have lived through so much together. Departing from friends like this is not done easily.

We finally packed the children into Denis's car and he drove us down the mountain. After looking for the staging area, driving back and forth for an hour, Denis found the designated place for Americans and dropped us off. The next four or five hours were madness.

Before I tell the story, I just want you to know that I am so grateful that the US Government is rescuing us. Kimarie and I both believe that this is above and beyond their duty. *Honestly.* We understood the risks of coming to live here and they told us in a traveler's advisory how dangerous it was and that we did so at our own risk. We accepted that responsibility for ourselves and didn't expect much of them. That having been said, I have to criticize the methods (or lack thereof) that they are using in the evacuation.

We crossed over an overpass bridge to a staging area with tents. No one was there to tell us what to do or where to stand. We figured out by asking people around us that the lines weren't moving because those who had gotten vouchers from the day before were walking to the front of the line and being processed first.

Around 1:00 PM, we overheard one of the US Marines on the other side of the razor wire give an estimated count of the people there, and then they pulled two trucks onto the bridge to block new people from joining us.

They sent out a guy with a red shirt and a weak bullhorn. It had a range of twenty feet. He instructed all the families with children to move *out of line* and follow him down to the sidewalk. It was explained later that this was to make the children more comfortable. We understood that the families with children were going to be prioritized.

An hour later Red Shirt came out with his bullhorn on the other side of the street *where* we *had been*, and shouted for families with three or more children to come. Unfortunately, no one could hear him from that range and so *everyone* charged over there with all their bags and children, pressing toward him. Without a line, those who were less mobile were seriously disadvantaged.

After a tense sorting process many families were designated to board the ship. In the midst of helpless people, I saw able-bodied families with four teenage children being prioritized over others that should have been taken first.

After awhile an amplified voice came from beyond the enclosure and announced that there was no more room. They would issue new vouchers so we could be prioritized tomorrow.

The five hundred to a thousand people remaining got irate and began shouting and mobbing poor Red Shirt. He reacted by moving to yet *another* area, causing *another* surge of the crowd. He got nervous that he would be crushed by the mob and shouted that we were all free to come back tomorrow, but that he *wasn't* going to give the vouchers! Everybody was in tears.

Eventually, other embassy workers *did* give out the vouchers, and the crowd dispersed to return to their various refuges.

We befriended a mother who was alone with her two small children in a double stroller. She had been there since 6:00 AM. She lacked mobility, and hadn't qualified for the cutoff of three children or more, so she didn't get on the ship. Her son has allergies and the special formula she just ran out of isn't available in Lebanon.

I saw another young woman with a full cast on her leg, weeping uncontrollably at the thought of suffering through the day for nothing. An old man, who was alone and could barely walk, was left sitting in a plastic chair someone had mercifully given him.

My heart is remakably heavy about today. I don't know if we will return tomorrow or wait for another day or two until things are better organized or until all the pushy people have had their way and the weaker ones have a chance.

Anyway, we are hearing that Cyprus is full up and having severe troubles handling all the refugees descending on them. There aren't enough planes to move them on from there. We heard that Americans were being put on chartered planes from Cyprus to Baltimore, but don't know if we should trust that. We also heard that we could be ferried to Turkey instead if Cyprus isn't able to cope.

I'll write more tomorrow and let you know what we decide, but right now we are feeling better about staying in a safe place here rather than becoming refugees in a country that doesn't have enough lodging space for us.

God is giving us grace; I should be much more exhausted than I am. I'm sure it will all catch up to me sooner or later.

Salaam,

Nate

Born In Tyre

One of the things Kimarie and I had to work through in our courtship negotiations was the number of children we planned to have. She always dreamed of having six. I thought two was better. I argued my case that the Eskimos' practice was to have only two so that if chased by a polar bear, each parent could grab one child and run, to ensure survival. We ended up agreeing on the perfect compromise of four, and Kimarie was pregnant a year after we were married.

Naomi was born in January of 2004. Her arrival signified another rebirthing experience for me in a long line of reformations. Knitting Kimarie and my lives together in marriage had meant becoming attuned to each others' preferences and conceding our interests to the point that we felt like we were giving up our individual identities. Having a baby shifted our focus even further away from ourselves and onto another little person's needs.

We decided that rather than flying to Europe for the birth, Kimarie would deliver in Lebanon, so our first task was to find an obstetrician. Our choices were narrowed thanks to Kimarie's preference for a woman doctor. We learned that we could choose from four in Tyre and interviewed them all to find their reaction to

Kimarie's intention of having an all-natural drug-free experience. We found exactly one who had been trained in Russia and was willing to follow the birth plan Kimarie had prepared.

Kimarie wanted me in attendance and to my surprise, I agreed – as long as I would only be responsible for working the north end. We ordered a 1970s Lamaze video online, and we watched it once, months before the due date. It was too hilarious to take seriously. The participants wore striped polyester leisure suits and one of the men sported a rainbow sweatband on his Caucasian Afro hairdo. We shut it off after the leader advised the women to visualize themselves as seabirds gliding above the water with wingtips just touching the surface of an imaginary lake. My training as a labor coach was extremely sparse.

Nine days before it was supposed to happen, Kimarie woke me up at 4:00 AM. Suddenly the growing lump that I had been talking to in-utero was going to come out and have something to say herself. For nine months I had repeated, "What'cha doin' in there? Why don't you come on out and play?" Well, today was the day. The time for abstract contemplation of what fatherhood would be like had slipped by quickly.

Every time a new groan followed a pause, I faithfully recorded the elapsed minutes on a small yellow legal pad. I emailed my parents the news that the first Scholz grandchild was forthcoming. I called and awoke the still travel-weary Wares in their hotel room at the Tyre Rest House, a few blocks away. Kimarie's parents got up, made their way to our apartment and arrived at 6:00 AM, just as Kimarie puked up her ill-advised breakfast. Throwing up was miserable, but she still preferred nausea to hunger.

As Kari helped her daughter put together an overnight bag to take to the hospital, I put the Lamaze video into the player out of desperation for some last minute advice. It was still playing when Kimarie announced it was time to go to the hospital. *Praise God for electricity to power the elevator!*

At the hospital, we had a private room assigned to us and when Kimarie learned she was still early in her labor, she reconsidered her plans for a drugless birth. To her great credit, Dr. Saliby talked her out of the change and encouraged her to stay the course. She left the two of us alone, and I tried to help my wife get comfortable.

Her back hurt. She figured out that if she could stretch it somehow, the pain subsided. We didn't have a medieval torture rack to stretch her out on and no hanging bars were installed in the doorway for nurses to do chin-ups in their spare time, so I got into position to comply with Kimarie's directions.

I was to stand on a chair, holding my arms straight out, and pull up on her wrists as she hung limp. It was in the following minutes that I came to respect the story of the battle between the Israelites and the Amalekites in the book of Exodus. The Israelites continued to win the battle in the valley below as long as Moses held his staff up above his head. But when his arms failed, the battle went against the Israelites (Exodus 17:11). I was desperate to help my wife overcome her pain, but if my supporting her full weight with my outstretched arms was what it took, it was clear that we were going to lose this battle.

Lamaze to the rescue! The concentration strategy that we had laughed about returned to Kimarie's memory and she began to control her pain by visualizing herself as an albatross, flapping her wings in time with her breathing, "sailing over the choppy ocean of her contractions below."

I stood by, attending to requests for ChapStick or sips of water, but careful not to disrupt her focus. It wasn't much later that her normal moaning in contractions was replaced by a different sound. It started as a low *Ö* sound, and rose in volume and pitch before ending in a laughing kind of whimper. Her experienced doctor father heard it from the waiting room and alerted the nursing staff that it was time.

She was promptly moved to the delivery room. Dr. Saliby shot me a doubtful glance as I walked in holding my wife's hand. I was permitted to attend the birth as long as I showed no signs of swooning. It was highly unusual for a husband to want to be in there. I put on my surgical mask and stretched the booties to the limit of their elasticity and managed to keep them from flying off the ends of my shoes.

It all happened quickly. Naomi was soon laid on her mother's chest, and the pain was forgotten.

Dr. Saliby stopped and motioned toward me with a funny-looking pair of scissors in her hand. "Do you want to cut the umbilical cord?"

She asked. We'd talked about this earlier, but she was checking to see if I'd changed my mind. "That's your job," I confirmed. Once disconnected, Naomi's slimy little body was wrapped in a blanket and handed to me. *So tiny.* "I'm glad you finally came out to play, little girl."

Before they took her away to meet her pediatrician and get cleaned up, I withdrew the indelible purple ink Sharpie pen from my pocket to implement my paranoid plan to ensure that our baby would not be switched by nefarious hospital baby-nappers. I pulled a squirming pink foot out of the blanket and wrote an "N" for Naomi on her heel. Then I reluctantly let her out of my sight for maybe five minutes before reuniting in the incubator room. In that short time, some nurse had scrubbed that initial off, probably relieved that it wasn't some sort of crazy birthmark. It had been silly to think that we wouldn't recognize her anyway.

Our stay in the hospital was short. Before we could leave I was expected to pay our hospital bill in full with cash. Kevin, Kimarie's father, went with me to the finance office on the ground floor. I barely tolerated the haze of cigarette smoke as I asked for my total, anxious to be gone. The hospital administrator began to explain something to me.

"Now we have to be careful, because sometimes insurance companies will visit us and so we have to be close. How much do you want me to make the paperwork out for?"

"Huh?" I grunted. I wasn't catching on. "How much do *I* want *you* to write it up for? How much did it cost?" *Was I expected to bargain for a cheaper price?*

"You owe the hospital $700 for your time here," he explained.

"Then charge me $700," I said impatiently. I was content to pay what I already thought was a low price without dickering.

The clerk was frustrated because I obviously didn't understand. He went to get help from his supervisor, who knew more English. The supervisor chose his words carefully, almost like a lawyer. It finally dawned on me that I was being invited to join the common Lebanese practice of insurance fraud by inflating the amount charged by the hospital in the billing documents.

I said, "I'm not going to do that. Make sure the billing correctly itemizes the $700 I'm paying you."

The original guy just stood there with his mouth hanging open like I had just told him I was a visitor from Mars. He looked imploringly at his boss as if to say, "Is this okay? I've never experienced this before. It's against normal protocol."

The supervisor smiled and authorized the man to proceed. He invited me to wait in his office over a glass of tea, while the paperwork was completed. He wanted to know how I had come to have such unusually high moral standards. In the weariness at the end of one of my longest days, I took the opportunity to describe what following Jesus meant to me.

As far as I know, Naomi was the first American born in Jebal Amal Hospital in Tyre.

In the next few days, all of our friends came to visit and sit with us and to meet the baby. Kevin and I rushed around in the car on the first day, acquiring gifts to honor both Eastern and Western traditions. We picked up the specially ornamented chocolates I had pre-ordered, and the pink and white Jordan almonds. They would be offered to visitors in a decorated pink box with a stuffed terrycloth lamb glued to its lid. To match this Lebanese convention, I decided to observe the archaic American ritual of handing out cigars. Kevin and I found a store in Sidon after a long search and bought twenty Cubans to hand out to visiting men.

Our neighbor Amina graciously cooked the dozens of bowls of cinnamon rice pudding, called *mughli*, that were customary to serve to our guests. I would disappear into the kitchen to prepare the bowls by sprinkling nuts and coconut on top. I also brewed the tea, while my in-laws tried to make small talk in the sitting room.

Kimarie's labor had ended, but mine was just beginning. It took a surprising amount of paperwork to have a baby in another country. An American birth was a rare enough occurrence in Tyre that the local authorities often scratched their heads wondering what forms they were supposed to ask for. Over the next five weeks, Denis, our lawyer, and I worked our way along the switchback paperwork trail that would lead to our being able to prove that Naomi was a Scholz and allow us to keep her.

We went to the city municipality building to initiate the forms.

Back to the hospital for the record of birth. To Dr. Saliby for her signature. Back to the municipality building to submit these forms and pay for an official stamp. Off to the General Security building, which is like the FBI and Immigration combined. Pay fees to a "fixer" to run the papers around to various desks in Beirut for signatures.

"Come back in two weeks to pick them up again," said the fixer.

On to the translator to make an English version and emboss it with his official seal. Prop the baby up for passport photos. Now we can take her with us on the hot two-hour car ride to the US Embassy, north of Beirut. Arrive at the Embassy early on Wednesday, which is the only day of the week to do this process. Take a number. Show a folder full of paperwork, including photos of a previously pregnant mommy and sonogram printouts.

"Oops. The passport photos you have aren't the right size. You'll have to go up the hill and get some more taken," said the embassy employee.

Off to try to prop up the baby for more photos. Back through the metal detectors and pat-downs at the embassy again.

"Okay. Pay your fees at the window at the end of the counter and then come back in two weeks to get Naomi's Certificate of Birth Abroad, her passport, and her Social Security number."

Another drive two weeks later and I was almost done. The last step was to bring her passport back to the General Security office to process her residence visa. Naomi came with me so I could show her to the official and prove she was real. It was one of the first times I took the baby out of the house on my own. I was nervous, but also excited to show her off.

We stepped into the cold, dark building and pushed through the crowds to the first office on our route. Naomi was an angel. For fifteen minutes, I filled out forms and pasted passport-sized photos into them. The last stop was to sit and wait our turn to get a signature on our documents from the officiating captain before the papers could be sent once again to Beirut for final processing and approval. I had spent a lot of time waiting in that office in the past. I dreaded the idea of sitting there in the cigarette smoke with a baby.

Just as I moved to take my place in line, Naomi had a stroke of genius and let out a bellowing wail. Everyone in the place turned to gape at the unlikely sight of a foreign man holding a screaming infant. In the tight quarters of the concrete-walled offices, her voice was amplified in a way that made the call to prayer seem like a whisper. I was rushed out of there and into the captain's waiting room. His executive assistant immediately jumped up from his desk. He grabbed Naomi's paperwork out of my hand, rushed past the dozen other people who were waiting, and into the inner office, re-emerging ten seconds later. By the time we were back in the car in the parking lot, Naomi had settled down to enjoy the drive home in peace.

A woman's tears, regardless of her age, serve as the finest tool known to mankind for cutting bureaucratic red tape. My smug approval of the abbreviated trip was tempered by the knowledge that this formidable weapon was likely to be used against me at some point in the future.

By April, we had all the documentation we needed to provide evidence that Naomi was ours, and we worked to integrate her into our lives. We discovered that we could still go out to the movies. Kimarie would put her in the Snuggli front-pack, and she would thrash all her extremities with excitement when we walked in and she saw the motion on the big screen.

Mel Gibson had made a movie about the Passion of Christ that I thought would never be allowed in our local theater. It was generally considered blasphemous to show a depiction of a prophet's face. But then it became big news that Jewish protestors demonstrated against the movie in the United States, calling the movie anti-Semitic. Arab Muslims in Lebanon wanted to see the show that had made the Jews so upset.

The cinema in Tyre had one screen. They usually changed the film every Thursday, unless it was a blockbuster that was sure to be well attended for another week. *The Passion of the Christ* was the only movie that had ever been held over for three weeks straight.

Kimarie and I went in the first week, and we brought Naomi with us. The filmmakers' decision to retain the original Aramaic language for the actors was awesome. The language was so similar to modern Arabic that I could tell most people in the audience didn't even have to read the subtitles. It was a good thing *we* knew the story pretty well though, because the subtitles were in French and Arabic.

The gory scenes were graphically disturbing, and I was glad Naomi fell asleep.

Despite the fact that Muslims strongly believe that Jesus was not crucified, people responded to the re-enactment. We had given the Muslim owner of the theater several boxes of Arabic New Testaments. His employees handed out the Bibles as gifts to Muslims leaving the theater in tears, just as emotional as I had seen them at the *majlis* during Ashura.

We left the theater in a daze that lasted for days. I was humbled. Our exaggerated surrender of self in parenthood contrasted poorly to Jesus' sacrifice.

Dear Family and Friends,

Many of you have responded to our intention not to try to board a ship today with strong pleas to go back and try. We considered that this morning. We decided to call another American family we were with yesterday, to see if they had returned to the port. They described the scene as being *fouda*, "chaos." Denis talked to them on the phone and could barely hear them over the noise of the crowd yelling from their end.

We were concerned several times *yesterday* that the situation would degenerate into a riot. Again, we have to evaluate risk and choose the path that minimizes it. We will wait until tomorrow, and try again.

In my estimation, the following things would eliminate the danger and greatly facilitate order at the staging area:

• One staff member with a counter at the entrance to the staging area. Stop taking people when the count matches their capacity for the day.

• Several staff members separating people who are arriving into needs and priority based sections. (e.g., sick/injured, with children, adults with no children)

• Section barricades with many staff members at each to answer questions and keep people calm.

• Distribution of an information sheet detailing the procedure they intend to implement so people know what to expect

• Install a public address system so that everyone can easily hear announcements

If anyone has access to a member of congress or the senate and is able to pass this information on to them, it might not be too late to help.

We have no idea how grueling the rest of our travels are likely to be after we are allowed on a boat, so we are attempting to get some extra rest today.

God bless you all. Thanks so much for your prayers.

Salaam,

Nate

THE BITTER DRINK

Mustafa pulled the metal shutters halfway down in front of the doors of his shop with a horrible scraping sound. I was passing by on my way to work, but I stopped and walked with him. We joined the approaching funeral procession moving down the middle of the street toward the cemetery a few blocks away.

Rattling metallic echoes followed as other businessmen in the neighborhood followed suit. Members of the community were expected to respect the dead, whether they knew the deceased or not. Death interrupted life in the city.

Nine or ten men shouldered a simple open wooden casket containing the remains, while a crowd converged behind them. The exertion of the burden grew overwhelming to one of the older pallbearers and he motioned with his free hand for another to take his place. The replacement scurried into position and they transitioned without interrupting the steady progress to the edge of town.

They turned left and through the cemetery gate, across from the pink feldspar pillars that were all that was left of the ancient Christian cathedral. A burial site had been prepared. The body was lifted from the box by family members pulling the corners of the cloth below it. Then they carefully lowered him into a raised marble box, positioned on his side, facing toward Mecca.

That evening, after helping Kimarie feed Naomi dinner, I went across the hall to Kamel's apartment to learn where the usbu'a was being held. Kamel always knew where. It was part of his business to rent the stacks of white plastic chairs that were needed. An *usbu'a* was like a wake that lasted for seven days.

"Let's go together," he said, and reached for his jacket.

I followed Kamel to the house. The door stood open and a group of men were just leaving. Everyone stood when we entered the room. The normal furniture had been moved out to make room for the ring of plastic chairs Kamel had provided. We started from the left, where the mourning family members sat closest to the door, shaking hands with everyone present. The men were free to take their seat once again after they greeted us. As I made the circuit, I repeated a consoling phrase Sadiq taught me, *Allah yirhamu*, "May God have mercy on him," to each one. Then I found an empty chair and sat down until the next guy came in.

The man sitting next to me picked up a silver tray from a small white plastic table and offered me a cigarette from an assortment of various brands. This was an occasion where smoking was encouraged.

"No thank you," I said.

The first time I went to an *usbu'a* was with Sadiq. I had been surprised at how many people were crowded into the house. "He must have been friends with everyone in town."

"No. He wasn't even a good man," Sadiq had confessed. "But that doesn't matter. It's our duty to go and show our respects and pray for the deceased. I certainly want people to come and pray for me when *I* die."

Visitors were offered bitter, unsugared coffee in tiny brown plastic cups. The teenagers of the family swarmed like bees, refilling cups. Taking a sip, I thought about Josey, who had helped me overcome my aversion to coffee. I had learned to tolerate it – even enjoy it, somewhat. I went through the suffering in advance for moments like these where I could share my friends' suffering appropriately.

After I left for Lebanon, Josey moved to Portland and became an iconic figure at a store called Blue Moon Camera. The last time I saw her was just a flash at my wedding reception. She had traveled for hours to be there, but it was impossible to catch up on old times in that kind of setting.

Two years later, on an icy Mother's Day, Josey was driving north to her hometown when her car hit a patch of black ice and spun off the freeway, coming to rest on the shoulder. Josey got out of the car to figure out what to do next and another driver slid on the same patch of ice and crushed her between the vehicles. She never regained consciousness and died in the hospital several days later.

Kamel and I talked a little, but conversation was subdued in favor of introspection. Every few minutes someone would shout, *'ul Fatiha*, "Say the Opening." The *Fatiha* prayer was the first chapter of the Koran and more commonly repeated in Islamic routine than the Lord's Prayer was by Christians. Conversation paused. Prayer beads rested across upturned palms as each man recited in barely audible whispers. Sadiq had helped me memorize and recite the words in Arabic.

> *In the name of God, The Compassionate, The Merciful*
> *Praise God – the Lord of the universe*
> *The Compassionate, The Merciful*
> *Ruler of the Day of Judgment*
> *You do we worship, and you do we call on for help*
> *Guide us along the Straight Path*
> *The path of those who you have favored*
> *Not of those who have angered you and gone astray*
> *Amen*

We prayed for mercy to be shown on the recently departed. It was our duty.

I took another swig of the coffee. The smell of coffee always made me picture my Dad's face. Dad drank his coffee a pot at a time.

He learned he had kidney cancer shortly after visiting me in Lebanon in the year of the Millennium. Surgeons removed the kidney and he was declared cancer-free for a time, but now, five years later, it showed up again and ravaged his bladder. My parents said that Kimarie and I should continue on in Tyre. *Did I do the right thing? Should I have gone back?*

I wrestled with my obligations to family and to what I felt God wanted from me. Was I kidding myself that our work here in Tyre was so important that I should deny my family our precious remaining time together? Or was I keeping my distance because I selfishly couldn't bear to witness Dad's slow deterioration?

Kimarie's second pregnancy advanced at seemingly the same pace that Dad weakened and neared death. How does one choose between attending the birth of a child or the death of a parent? The Bible says God never gives us more than we can handle, but from my perspective, it sometimes seemed like I was a better judge of my limits than he was.

Kamel nudged my leg. We had stayed the obligatory half hour and it was now socially acceptable for us to stand and make our exit. Everyone stood again as we circled the hand shaking loop once more.

"May God have mercy on him."

***

It turned out I didn't have to choose. Gideon was born at the same hospital with the same doctor and grandparents in attendance as Naomi was – sixteen months after her. Parenthood had already sunk into Kimarie and me, but Naomi had never been a big sister. When we brought Gideon home to her, she couldn't stop giggling. She pulled his sock off, saw his tiny foot wiggling and laughed with delight. It was love at first sight. I went right to work pushing papers.

Three weeks after Gideon was born I got the phone call from Mom. "The hospice nurse says he will die soon. Please come as quickly as you can."

I immediately made travel arrangements and began my journey the next day. The best routing I could book on such short notice required me to spend thirty hours traveling: three flights and two layovers. I normally relished thinking time to myself, but this was torture. The last time I saw Dad, he looked healthy. Reports from my brother, who had visited more recently, told of his rapidly declining condition.

I sat waiting for a plane at my gate in the Detroit airport in a stupor of foreboding.

My trance was broken when a covered Arab woman walked past. I recognized her from the first two flights we'd shared from Beirut. It seemed like we were on parallel courses. She wore a confused look on her face and scanned the walls, back and forth, before slipping through the door to the jet way. The airline staff freaked out. Two ladies chased her down, shouting. When they came back out of the door, they looked ready to have her arrested for terrorist activity. She spoke frantically in Arabic, but they couldn't understand. I hopped up and went over to see if I could help.

I said, *"Fini sa'idik shi, amti? Shu maelik?"*

It turned out she needed a restroom and couldn't read the signs. We pointed her in the right direction and she hurried away thankfully. The funny part was the slack-jawed looks directed at me by onlookers as I returned to my seat. I saw the fear of a seemingly scary situation, mixed with the shock of the white guy speaking Arabic and saving the day. I felt like tipping my hat and saying "all in a day's work ma'am," in a Southern accent.

I don't remember how I got from the airport to my parents' house. Maybe Mom picked me up from the ferry dock. It was 2:00 AM. I was exhausted from Gideon's citizenship paperwork and travel weary from my trip, but before I could rest I had to see Dad. *This could be my only chance.*

The hospice caregiver ushered me in to my parents' room. Their bed had been replaced with a mechanical hospital bed. My dad was lying under a thin sheet; the oxygen tube ran below his nose. He had been transformed from the healthy, muscular man I knew as my father, into a version that might have been found in a concentration camp in Nazi Germany. He sweated from the exertion of staying alive. He was mostly incoherent, either from pain or from the drugs, but I saw that he recognized me and was grateful I had come. I sat with him, held his hand for a while before finally heading to bed. I had seldom been that tired, but my sleep was still disrupted with dread. I wondered if he would survive the night.

The next morning he was still there and more lucid. I described the birth of his new grandson. Gideon was the firstborn Scholz boy of his generation. Dad had only sisters. I had produced an heir to preserve the family name.

He labored to communicate, but managed a dry whisper, "Carry on."

Later that morning, Mom and I took care of some business at the department of licensing in town. We transferred the title of Dad's 1965 Ford Mustang over to me. He had sold it to me long ago, but we had neglected to finalize the paperwork. When he'd announced his intentions to get rid of it, I couldn't bear the idea of letting it go to a stranger. I learned to drive in that car. Kimarie and I drove it away from our wedding. Dad had purchased it brand new a few weeks before I was born.

On the way home, Mom mentioned she wanted me to spend some time assessing a project downstairs. After Dad retired from his teaching career, he had become a dealer of antiques. When he became too sick to work at it, his unsold inventory was stowed into boxes and stacked against the dank walls in the basement. I creaked down the stairs to poke around. Soon the task would fall to me to help Mom get rid of this stuff. Mostly, I found books: author inscribed, first editions, or just plain old. Aside from the books was an odd assortment of locking cast-iron piggy banks, PEZ dispensers, hydroplane memorabilia, antique toys and puzzles. I grabbed an old wooden box from the top of a stack of cardboard boxes. I slid the recessed lid to the side and found it packed full of yo-yos in all different colors and sizes and kinds.

Really? Yo-yos? There was a time when having a yo-yo had been significant to me.

When I was in Cub Scouts our annual fundraiser activity was to sell tickets for admission to the Cub Scout Jamboree, which was held in some crazy place like Kentucky, three thousand miles away. We didn't get to sell anything as desirable as cookies, like the Girl Scouts did. The tickets were only a dollar apiece, but assuming anyone had wanted to attend the Jamboree, it would have cost them several hundred dollars more to travel there. Clearly, we relied on our neighbors' sense of pity to move the worthless tickets we peddled.

Boys were rewarded on the basis of the number of tickets they sold. The troop leaders sent home a catalog early in the process to motivate us, filled with cool camping gear guaranteed to make boys drool. It made the Sears Christmas Wish Book look uninteresting. I think the minimum number of tickets sold to earn the smallest prize was five. Some of the treasures in the back pages of the magazine required the sale of hundreds of tickets. The Cubs were allowed to choose how to spend their commission. The prizes were ordered by the scoutmaster and then awarded publicly at the final full pack meeting in the grade-school auditorium at the end of the school year.

The folks within walking distance of my house already knew me as the door-to-door seller of wild blackberries and daffodils, so I had worn out my neighbors' capacity for the pity sale. Despite my sore feet and canvassing efforts I failed to sell the minimum number of tickets to receive the most token of prizes at the awards ceremony: a yellow yo-yo with a Cub Scout decal on the side. I went to the pack meeting with a sinking spirit. Somehow many of the boys that year had managed to con family and friends out of enough dollars to warrant some upper end gifts. I guess my parents hadn't thought to help me sell them, or at least buy the $5 of tickets it would have taken to get something. Truthfully, on my dad's meager teacher's salary, they might not have been able to afford to help.

As I watched the distribution of prizes, knowing I would get nothing, I began to feel more and more disappointed in myself. By the time I got home I had grown so ashamed that my chest tightened and the corners of my mouth uncontrollably twitched downward. I made it to bed upstairs before the floodgates roared out of control. It took awhile for my folks to notice I was crying.

When dad came up to find out what was wrong he was bewildered at the level of emotional turmoil I had reached. I was locked in an internal interrogation about my self-worth. *I'm a failure. I couldn't even sell enough tickets to earn a stupid yo-yo.* He promised to take me shopping at the drugstore the next day and I calmed down enough to fall asleep. The next morning, true to his word, my dad went with me to spend money he didn't have to spare on a yo-yo for his son.

I closed up the yo-yo box and went upstairs to join the other family members chatting in the living room. The hospice care provider had cleared out during the day as usual, so Mom went in frequently to see if Dad needed anything. At around noon, she came from the bedroom white-faced and trembling, "I think your father just died."

I felt my own countenance change as I got up to confirm what Mom thought. I checked his pulse and laid my head on his bare chest to listen for a heartbeat. He felt warm with perspiration, but silent and still. The patriarchal mantle passed to me and I found it instantly heavy.

"Good-bye, dad," was all I could manage to say.

***

When the first son is born into a middle-eastern family the father's level of respect in the community rises. Both my identity and name changed to reflect my son's arrival. The nickname for Gideon in Arabic

159

is *Jad*, so I became known as *Abu Jad*, "Father of Gideon." He wasn't named after me. I was re-named after him.

But it worked differently in the West. Identity was in the family name passed from father to son. Through Gideon and Elijah and Zadek the legacy of *Scholz* will, in my father's words:

"Carry on."

From: Nate Scholz
Sent: Friday, July 21, 2006
Subject: Day 10 — Evening

All right, so we said that we weren't going to go down today. Well, we did, but a little too late. Another family from the monastery went down in the morning, gave up, and came back around noon. They told us changes had been made, so we decided to give it a shot. But by the tlme we got there, the trucks had been moved into their blocking position and everyone was dispersing.

There is now a new entrance before reaching the staging area. They're giving no preferential treatment for vouchers at this first opening, so the ugliness and pressing of people is just as bad there as it was before. Once people get through that gate, though, it seems that those who have vouchers are insured a spot on the boat, so people are calming down considerably beyond that. Not completely sure, but that's what we could gather.

We have re-prioritized our remaining belongings and repacked to create better mobility. We will carry two backpacks and one small duffel bag. These contain my computer, our baby books, a change of clothes, and some food and diapers. For those of you who have hosted us in the past, you know it is nothing short of a miracle for us to travel so light.

We believe that we will get up early tomorrow and try to arrive at the port around 7:00 AM. We pray that the crowd will be a little lighter at that time and that our vouchers will get us on an early boat. At this point we don't know where we will be routed beyond that, but we believe that the government is committed to getting us to Baltimore.

Please pray for the Holy Spirit to descend on the people tomorrow and comfort and calm everyone, and of course that we will get on a boat...

Salaam,

Nate

Hezbollah Rally

The atmosphere was electric. It was April 2006, and preparations for a Hezbollah political rally had been going on for weeks. Security was tight. It was to be the first public speech of Hassan Nasrallah ever held in the Shia city of Tyre. I felt compelled to go and pray for him.

"If I don't get going now, I'll be too late to get a seat," I told Kimarie. "I'm going to have to walk the whole way because I'm sure all the roads will be closed. Even if they're not, I don't want to be out there in the traffic jam."

Kimarie answered, "Okay. Have fun. I'll probably just stay cool with the kids here in the pool on the balcony. Dinner will be ready at six."

I gave Naomi and Gideon each a squeeze and kissed my wife as I headed for the door. I didn't have an ounce of hesitation. It was a community event and I had been part of the community for nearly seven years. Over the previous week when I had mentioned my plans to go to the event, none of my neighbors or friends had given any hint of caution for my safety.

My shirt already stuck to my back. Humidity was a fact of life that just had to be tolerated. I meandered along the beach, heading toward the hole in the fence around the chariot track. The direct path of cutting through the ruins took at least half a mile off my route. I once again enjoyed the sense of serenity at my holy place. I made my way around weather-pocked pillars that once supported the aqueduct, carrying life-giving water to the citizens of ancient Tyre. Weeds threatened to cover the tombs in the necropolis along the Byzantine road.

At the main entrance to the hippodrome, I greeted the old friends who had given me permission to use the hole as a shortcut. When I told them I was headed for the rally, the look on their faces gave me a clue that maybe it wasn't such a good idea after all.

Hezbollah had a history of kidnapping Westerners, but Nasrallah himself repeated publicly that the Muslims of Lebanon carried no hostility toward individual Americans. Their frustrations were with America's politicians and its foreign policy.

I tried to push the new doubts out of my mind and after assuring my friends that I would be fine, I continued on my way. I emerged from the gate onto the main coastal highway that ran from Beirut in the north to the border with Israel in the south. It was the first time I had ever seen it closed to traffic. Instead, it had become a channel for a river of people flowing down from side roads. Everyone wore black.

As I merged into the rapids, I fell in behind a couple of women wearing head-coverings and leading their children. One of the little girls wore a red baseball cap turned backward on her head. I smiled to myself as I read the slogan printed on the bill of her cap bouncing lightly in front of me. "I ♥ Jesus." My expectancy grew that God had planned something big for the day.

Despite the predominant color being black and the likelihood that the speech would be another opportunity to spout menacing, saber-rattling rhetoric, a lighthearted attitude was shared in the crowd as we moved northward. Roadside entrepreneurs set up their carts and sold cotton candy, balloons, and ice cream, which made the gathering feel oddly similar to the annual Vashon Island Strawberry Festival parade.

I passed the al-Bass traffic circle and continued north. Hezbollah fighters on the sidewalk scanned the swarming people for irregularities suggesting a security breach. Long metal barricades with vertical bars stood in concrete blocks along the edges of the road. At first the artificial paths they had created were as wide as the street and I continued to mill along in the center of the crowd, invisible – anonymous. The railings gradually narrowed to help control the foot traffic. The sensation was so much like being herded, that I was tempted to "moo" as I was shuffled through the gates. Thankfully, I resisted the urge.

Up ahead, the density of the crowd increased. I couldn't believe what I was seeing. *This is a lot more people than I expected to be here.* I resumed feeling nervous.

I was close to an Arab Christian friend's house, on the same street. I decided it would be a good idea to get a better look of what was up ahead from his fourth floor balcony. I was about two blocks away from the rally when I arrived at his building. An armed Hezbollah militiaman stood on the front steps watching the crowd moving by. I blithely ignored him and bounded up the stairs and through the open front door, heading for the elevator in the lobby.

"Stop! Come back here!" he ordered. I froze, surprised. He was watching the crowd, but his main job was to control the security of this building. I'm sure he never guessed he'd encounter a Westerner within a hundred miles of this event. Here I was walking into the building for which he was responsible. I had his full attention. The investigation began.

"Who are you, and what are you doing here? Do you live in this building?" The guy barked in Arabic. He advanced toward me with the authority of square-jawed, hard-muscled militancy.

"My name is Nate, but everyone calls me Abu Jad. I am visiting a friend in the building. Isn't that okay?" I replied in a steady, but compliant tone.

"What is your nationality?"

"I'm an American." His eyebrows shot up at my response. *What's going to happen now? Am I about to be taken away for interrogation?*

Instead of escalating tensions, my answer surprisingly calmed him down. More softly, he asked, "Who's your friend? Which floor does he live on?"

"His name is Edmond. He lives on the fourth floor."

"What's his phone number?"

I consulted my Nokia, hit the call button and explained to Edmond what was going on before handing it to the reaching hand of the soldier. He confirmed with Edmond that I was expected to visit, closed the connection, and handed the phone back to me. When he spoke into his two-way radio to report what was going on, his left hand still held his assault rifle.

The exchange moved from cross-examination to conversation. He was still intrigued. "Where did you learn to speak Arabic?"

"I've lived here in Tyre for close to seven years. Mostly, I learned from people like you on the street, but I also took classes at the language center in Hay Ramel. I teach conversational English there."

"I'm sorry to have troubled you. Thank you for your patience. This is an important event and we have to be very careful with security."

I barely kept my mouth from falling open and replied, "I understand. It's not a problem."

"You're welcome. Enjoy your visit."

Alone in the elevator, I shook my head in disbelief. I didn't think my friends in the States would ever believe this story. *How do I get myself into situations like this?*

Edmond met me at the elevator and I apologized for drawing unwanted attention to him. We surveyed the view of the street together from his balcony.

About a mile and a half from the old city of Tyre, in the outlying neighborhood between the suburbs of al-Bass and Abbassieh, was a suitable empty lot for a political rally with a controlled line of sight with all the surrounding buildings. For weeks, workers had cleared away brush, scrap metal, and the usual garbage that finds its way to empty urban places. Heavy equipment had filled holes and leveled hills. For days, others had transported white, red, and yellow plastic chairs and arranged them neatly into countless rows.

The sea of people was impressive. They walked on the main road through the south, which meant that many of these people from out of town had parked a long distance away. Many of them must have walked miles, judging by the immensity of the crowd.

Nasrallah became secretary general of Hezbollah in 1992 when his predecessor was assassinated. Nasrallah was a legitimate political leader in the Lebanese government. Clearly, his popularity still rode on the expulsion of the Israeli occupation. His speech was due to start in fifteen minutes.

We couldn't see the stage. It was backed up to the side of a building that faced away from us. We could just see a sliver of the seating area, but had an open view of the mile of bobbing heads where the city streets had been. The multitude compacted and movement ceased as the crowd approached the spectator yard. The event site had already reached capacity, and those who had not arrived early were left to fight for a position within earshot of the enormous speakers.

I resigned myself to pray from this balcony and watch the televised coverage from Edmond's apartment. He didn't want me to go anyway. He thought I was crazy to have risked coming this far. If I went, I would only attract more attention that could later cause me grief.

Was I being stupid? Could I just decide that the world's media sources were wrong about Hezbollah – that I alone understood that they had changed from their chaotic formative years and were currently misjudged? It was like an African American trusting in a kinder, gentler Ku Klux Klan, and joining a midnight skinhead meeting. *What gave me such confidence to boldly trust in a course of action that was so obviously foolish to everyone else?*

I had just made friendly conversation with a Hezbollah militiaman. I was in the act of praying for a guy my country considered to be the leader of a terrorist organization. *Could the Department of Homeland Security count prayer as "offering aid to an enemy of the state?"* Some people might call me a traitor for teaching English to Muslims. *Still, I had such a strong impulse to do this.*

Edmond was one of those people I most admired, who prayed regularly. For hours a day he worked his way around the string of prayer beads commonly carried by Muslims and Christians alike. He paced back and forth on his marble balcony floor and cried out for the needs of individual people and for God's glory to be known among the nations. That day I almost matched his intensity.

I wanted to be there to be a part of whatever God was going to do, to be a witness. I was convinced that God was going to reveal himself in some dramatic way. I imagined a scene playing out like in the movies: a perfectly circular opening forming in the overhead clouds and a beam of light pouring down through it with God's booming voice directing the entire Shia Muslim population to follow Jesus. I expected God to clarify that Jesus was the *straight path* they kept asking him to reveal. The sense of attentive expectation stayed with me as I watched the live footage on the television.

The Hezbollah chairman delivered his speech while the cameras panned across the faces of evangelical pastors, Maronite Catholic priests, Sunni imams, and Shia sayyids. Politics and religion were fused in Lebanon, so all the religious leaders of the South had been invited to sit on the stage next to the podium. The opportunity was too prestigious to pass up, and absence could have repercussions.

The massive crowd of people looked for a word of hope from their leader. Would their lives improve? Or were they destined to suffer in a permanent state of fear amidst a troubled economy, discriminated against by the distant Christian and Sunni power brokers of government in Beirut? What an opportune moment for God to show himself in a mass epiphany. I walked aimlessly around the room and prayed with prophetic imagination, inspired by the potential of the moment.

Edmond sat for over an hour in rapt attention to the formal Arabic I couldn't understand. I alternated between the balcony and the living room, in constant motion.

Eventually, the speech ended and Edmond stood up. His face was non-expressive.

"What happened?" I asked.

"He didn't say anything new. It was the same old message as always."

The crowd dispersed – no epiphanies. There had been no clouds available in the sky to part for dramatic effect. I had been so sure that something unusual and powerful would happen that I plopped down on the green, wool couch with a confused look and just sat there for another hour. I was convinced I hadn't wasted my time. Still, I had expected to be gratified by witnessing the result for which I had prayed.

Kimarie would have dinner ready soon. I thanked Edmond and his wife for their hospitality and returned to the street. The crowds and the militia were already gone. Halfway home, I walked around the lowered gate into the chariot track parking lot. The caretakers had gone home for the day. A truncated pillar, sticking up like a tree stump, enticed me to sit and think awhile longer.

The anticlimactic day was tolerable, but what about the last seven years? Kimarie and I had recently felt God releasing us to move on. Denis was reluctant to let us go, and the idea of leaving was hard for us, too. But Mom needed our help, and I believed I was best suited to applying myself toward helping fellow Americans overcome their fear of Muslims. A change of calling can be as hard to discern as initially identifying one. We planned to continue on in Tyre until the end of the year before moving back to the Seattle area.

A nagging thought pestered me: *I want more to show for the prime time of my thirties spent here.* I had envisioned the hippodrome crammed with thousands of Shia followers of Jesus, worshipping together – but that had not materialized. We were excited about the growing numbers of new believers discipling others in their own social circles. But was that enough to justify the sacrifices?

Somewhere I had gotten the idea that my obedience to God's call earned me the right to produce the results I expected. I wanted God to resolve everything into a tidy understandable package. But that's not how God is. He is compassionate, merciful, good – but unbridled. He gets to decide what is worth spending my life on.

Nasrallah may have been completely unaffected by my prayers that day. God may have just wanted to spend the time with me. Or maybe my prayers had some effect on the war that would break out two months later and cut short our stay in Lebanon. Maybe someday God will fill me in on what really happened.

CONVERGENCE

We made good progress on the open road until we reached the Litani River. Kimarie was next to me in the passenger seat of our Mitsubishi SUV, the kids in their car seats behind us. Denis led the small, two car caravan in his Honda van with his and Edmond's family. The bridge over the Litani had been destroyed five days earlier on the first day of the war.

On normal days, this stretch of road was just wide enough for two-way traffic with some passing capability. That day, however, it held four to six lanes of northbound traffic and another lane merging from a large arterial street emptying out of the village of Bourj Rahal up the hill. We moved a car length every five minutes and bumpers occasionally touched. Crowding that extra inch seemed crucial. It was impossible to tell what awaited us ahead or why the cars weren't moving forward.

My scalp prickled at the sound of jets overhead. Our car was trapped so tightly in its place that we couldn't open the doors. Everything inside me irrationally told me to roll down the window and pull my family out of the car. Thirty feet away from us stood one of the few unbombed gas stations remaining in the South.

Kimarie and I looked at each other. I didn't need to explain it to her.

Where were the reassuring little white butterflies when we needed them?

Twenty minutes later, the reason we had stopped became clear. A string of taxi-vans appeared ahead, wrestling against the stream of traffic. Motorists miraculously worked together, and jockeyed their vehicles into odd angles to solve the puzzle of creating space. The taxi drivers were heading back to the Rest House Hotel in Tyre, braving the roads to transport high-paying passengers up to Beirut.

After they squeaked by us, the traffic started moving again and we let out our breath as we pulled away from the gas station. Just before the ruined bridge, we turned right and snaked along the south bank of the river, following its contours. A narrow orchard road lined with orange trees served as a detour for a couple of miles.

An old sedan in front of Denis's car overheated and stopped, blocking traffic again. The driver jumped out and raised his hood. Denis offered him a bottle of water to pour into his radiator, and the car was coaxed once more into motion.

We finally reached a narrow spot in the river where an emergency crossing had been hastily constructed with a corrugated storm drainpipe covered in dirt. Army officers and civilians stood at the corner before the causeway, risking their lives directing traffic. It was quite a relief when we finally made it over to the other side. *One more river to go between us and safety.*

Just then we saw our neighbor from the twelfth floor standing on the side of the road! I rolled down the window as we drove by, and shouted, "Hey, Abu Omar! Are you okay?"

He gave a thin smile, "Yes, praise God. I'm waiting for Kamel. He's close behind you in my Mercedes with our families. We're going to stay with my relatives in Damascus."

We were glad to hear that they were also headed to a safer place.

We turned left again toward the main road, and plodded a car length at a time for too long. Traffic thinned once we got back to the coastal highway. The white sheet I had duct-taped to the roof of the car flapped wildly, as if to say, "Please don't shoot us. We're just trying to get out of here!" We raced north toward unknown obstacles.

The haggard residents of the village of Sarafand sat alongside the road in plastic chairs. A parade of refugees coursing through their neighborhoods as the villagers watched with glazed expressions, like unemployed people-watchers in a shopping mall.

As we neared the torn oil storage tanks at Zahrani, the sky turned dark with the smoke that billowed from the gigantic iron hulls. We poked our way beneath the caved-in remnants of the main freeway interchange between inland Nabatieh and the coast road, on which construction had only recently been completed.

Denis knew of an alternate crossing for the Awali River. We knew better than to assume that the bridge on the main highway would be usable. He followed crude cardboard signs that had been propped against trees by the road to direct escapees to the right route. I didn't know where we were.

"It makes me nervous that there's no other traffic around. If we're going the right way, shouldn't there be traffic?" I worried to Kimarie. "See if you can call Denis to make sure he knows where we're going?"

She picked up the phone from the dashboard tray and speed-dialed. "There's still no signal," she reported. "It's probably fine. I trust Denis, and we keep passing those signs."

A white van and a red car came careening around a corner from the direction we were headed. A wild-eyed teenager waved out the car's window to attract our attention and shouted, *Rajaou, rajaou!* "Go back!"

I glanced over at Denis's car to get my cue for what to do. When I saw a hint of his intention to turn around, I rapidly executed a three-point turn and zoomed the quarter mile back to the last intersection we had passed. We pieced together from the news that evening that the small bridge we had been about to cross was bombed and destroyed just moments before we were diverted. Ten people died.

As I waited for Denis to catch up to us, I glanced at my kids in the back seat. When I came to Lebanon as a single young man, I had counted the cost of being a disciple of Jesus and was ready, in a romantically idealistic way, to give up my life. After I got married, I accepted the same potential cost for my bride, who also made her own decision. My children had made no such choice. *Am I willing to trust God's wild will for them? How could I live with myself if one of them was killed?*

Denis pulled to the side of the road and got out to confer with us. "What took you so long?" I asked.

"I stopped for a second to look a little farther down the road. I saw a car down there with the driver's door twisted up like a ripped soda can," he said, stress written across his face. "Did you see the guy in the van with blood all over his face?"

Denis again took the lead and trail-blazed on unexplored roads. We would have to try getting past the river by going up and around. We weren't sure if the road would be blocked, but it was our last option. It took fifteen tense minutes of zigzagging to rejoin the crowds of fleeing refugees on the more familiar road to Jezzine. It was there at the waterfall that we would be able to cross the Awali near its source. After two more hours of driving, we began to feel safer.

We passed through a deserted valley below a freeway overpass, part of the road to Damascus, Syria. I slowed our driving pace and we craned our necks to examine the span, far above us. Directly overhead, the light of day shone through the grid-work pattern of rebar remaining in the eastbound lanes of the broken backbone of a bridge.

Kimarie sighed deeply and shook her head. "Everything this country has spent so much effort on rebuilding since the civil war has been destroyed again." I thought of the sound of jets overhead, the smoking oil tanks at Zahrani. "The clock has been turned back ten years," Kimarie continued, "and if this keeps up, it'll turn back twenty. So much lost. Peace, progress, lives…"

As we left the shadow of the bridge behind us, Kimarie fell back into her seat and looked straight ahead. When I glanced over, I saw her face was etched with grief.

Dear Family and Friends,

We arrived at the staging area to try to get on the ship at about 7:00 AM yesterday. The vouchers we'd been given earlier didn't do us any good, but the improvement in the system for moving people efficiently was dramatic. People announced info at every stage. We were given shade. The line stayed a line and moved linearly.

By 1:00 PM we had been screened at a makeshift customs station, registered and loaded on buses, and driven to the Orient Queen cruise liner. We were assigned a small but nice cabin and departed for Limassol. We tried to call Denis to let him know we were on board, but he didn't answer his phone.

About an hour later, he called and told us that the radio towers adjacent to the monastery we were staying in had been bombed! The blast blew out windows, but only one man was injured with some cuts. Needless to say, our group was traumatized again by the third close hit.

We stayed the night on board the Orient Queen, whose crew and staff hadn't slept for days after volunteering to help the US government evacuate us. You could tell they were haggard, but continued to be helpful.

This morning we had a hard time getting off the vessel because they didn't organize our disembarking. After the announcement was made through the ship's intercom speakers that we could get off the ship, we all rushed the gangplank at the same moment. People crowded through the maze of corridors without knowing which direction to exit.

After we got off the boat, we went through immigration and customs and boarded buses bound for Nicosia. We are in Nicosia now. We'll continue to keep you posted as we are able, but it is more difficult now that we are on the road.

Salaam,

Nate

REFUGEES

From the gangplank off the ship at the port of Limassol, we were led across the wharf and into a reception building. We separated and I lined up to register with our passports while Kimarie sat in the waiting area with the kids. I chose a cordoned line that turned out to be the slow lane – just like at the grocery store. When I reached the ubiquitous official with the laptop, he checked us off his list. "Is the airport nearby?" I asked. "Which airport will we be landing at in the States?"

He answered mechanically, "You won't be getting on a plane right away. A bus will take you to the fairgrounds to wait until a flight can be arranged. I can't tell you where you'll land. It could be anywhere on the East Coast." I'm sure he'd answered the same question a thousand times already.

I went back to find Kimarie crying, by herself.

"What's wrong? Where are the kids?" My mind raced to worst case scenarios as usual. She pointed to a small nursery area where our children played, and wiped her eyes before answering.

"I went to the relief station over there to see what they had. When that woman gave me some milk for Gideon, I just fell apart. I've handed out meals to homeless people in Seattle before, but never expected to be on the receiving end." I put my arm around Kimarie's shoulders and shielded her so she could have a good cry – just the two of us in a room full of people.

When she was collected again, we picked up the kids, headed out of the building, and tried to guess which of the buses would leave first. We boarded one and waited for all the seats to be filled, then spent an hour riding to the Cyprus International fairgrounds in Nicosia. We were added to the thousands of others waiting in the evacuee center hosted by the United States Marine Corps, who had moved heaven and earth to transform the site into a safe haven for us. We were to expect to be their guests for at least twenty-four hours.

Several gigantic buildings formed a campus like any other fairgrounds. We went directly to one of the massive sleeping areas in a sheet metal covered hangar. We were issued bedding, towels, food, water, and more diapers – all the necessities. It was way too hot. The ridiculously small fan-blades on the thirty-foot ceiling spun lazily in a feeble attempt to circulate the air. From below, we felt no effect. Even the shade of the few trees outside offered little relief from the heavy humidity. I found a likely cluster of cots while Kimarie took a turn splitting off to line up at another building with our passports to register us again.

We spent much of that day trying to stay as still as possible to avoid sweating, but the kids whined and flopped and required us to chase them around. We ate dinner from olive green foil pouches that magically cooked the food inside after we added water.

The lights were never turned off in our quarters. It was a trial to get the children to sleep with people talking and walking all around them, but they eventually drifted off. The cots creaked loudly when anyone rolled over. With so many of us packed together in one place, the constant sound reminded me of the frog pond behind my parents' house.

A family with six older kids had parked themselves next to us. They played cards and were generally noisy until well after dark. I lay on my back, dozing and watching the rats ambling along the rafters. Every few hours in the middle of the night the PA blasted a long list of the names of people whose turn it was to go to the airport. Half awake we strained to hear our names with groggy minds and then re-attempted sleep when they weren't called.

The children predictably woke early, and it was our turn to disturb the slumber of others. Bassam was the father of the family next to us. He came back from an early morning exploration with some great information.

"I found a hidden cafe on the other side of the fairgrounds. They'll cook you breakfast to order off a menu."

"And you don't have to pay?" I asked.

"Right. It's free – and it's nearly empty this early in the morning. You can sit and relax with no crowds."

The cafe was out of earshot of the loudspeakers, but the coffee was good and the seating was comfortable. After breakfast, the kids played in a courtyard nearby in the cool of the morning, but I grew nervous that our names had been called in our absence and we went back to our cot fortress.

At about 9:30 AM, a crackly voice read "Scholz" over the loudspeaker in the list of names. Lines. Registration. Directions. Board one of two dozen buses bound for one of several possible airports, then get on a plane to an undisclosed East Coast American city.

"Which airport are you going to?" I asked one of the bus drivers from below the stairs.

He shrugged and said, "I don't know. Just get on the bus and we'll take you somewhere." The driver also waited for a last minute assignment before he pulled away from the parking lot. I don't think the Marines even knew where each person would be going until they got to their destination and checked in at registration again. The duration of our stay in the fairgrounds at Nicosia was just about twenty-four hours, as the Marines had predicted.

Naomi spent the time watching out the window of the bus for dump trucks and backhoes. She was obsessed with finding a backhoe of every different color she could name, and she pretty much *did* find them: red, yellow, orange, green, and blue.

Construction sites bustled everywhere. Cyprus was booming. Buildings rose almost as fast as they had fallen in Lebanon. Roadwork stopped our progress, and we waited. The heavy equipment moved out of the way, and the flow resumed again. Our driver whisked us through the regular life around us – a caravan of displaced persons, quarantined behind heavily tinted windows.

We eventually arrived at Paphos International Airport, on the farthest side of the island from the port of Limassol, where we'd been deposited by the Orient Queen. After an additional round of processing at the airport, we were given boarding passes and led to a waiting room to sit for another couple of hours. The kids' behavior degenerated. Kimarie and I exhausted what little reserves of energy we had left in keeping them corralled. They threw food, played in the ashtrays, and ran shouting down the crowded narrow aisles of airport seating, jostling the other beleaguered travelers who gave us that disapproving look reserved for delinquent parents.

We were overjoyed to get on the chartered World Airways plane bound for Philadelphia. We learned we would have a brief stop in Rome for refueling, and it wasn't long before we were landing in Italy.

In Rome, we expected to stay on the plane for an hour and a half, but because of problems with catering trays being the wrong size for the food carts, the wait was extended to three hours. We weren't allowed to leave our seats. The sun beat on the shell of the plane. Nobody likes being confined in a tight space with no air circulation, but Lebanese people are more prone to feeling claustrophobic as a general rule. The majority of passengers were Lebanese-born Americans, and their frightened eyes revealed barely controlled panic.

I had been seated right in front of a kid whose legs were the perfect length to continually kick me in the small of the back. The cumulative hours of sitting, with no resources to entertain our one and two-year-olds, had pushed us to an indescribable level of discomfort. Even the flight attendants gave up trying to mask their misery.

Once we were airborn, Kimarie made an effort to get the children comfortable in the three seats we had been given for the four of us. She laid one of them down on the seat and stretched out on the floor with the other. It wasn't long before a flight attendant came along and interrupted our momentary serenity.

"Ma'am, you're going to need to get back up and buckle your lap belt," she said firmly. "We can't have you lying on the floor."

"Why not?" Kimarie was not in the mood for being told to follow rules. "This is the only way we can get these kids comfortable, and they need to sleep."

"I understand that, but it's against FAA regulations. It would be very dangerous for you if we hit turbulence. You could be thrown up against the ceiling."

That unlikely danger seemed trivial compared to what we'd just gone through. Kimarie joylessly complied. I wearily watched whatever movie played, without earphones.

By the time we reached Philadelphia, we had been on the plane fourteen hours.

Customs moved quickly for us because we had no checked bags. The United States had done their part to get us back in the country. Our evacuation was officially over and we would have to find our own way home from here. However, the American Red Cross knew we were coming, and aid workers had prepared a staging area to serve us. A nice older guy handled all our needs personally. He went with Gideon and Kimarie when we split up to tackle different projects. They worked on booking a flight from Philadelphia to Seattle. I kept Naomi with me and went to another desk to arrange for a motel room.

Volunteers stood behind long tables stacked with clothes and needed supplies. They gave us books and stuffed Mickey Mouses for the children. I was humbled to take a fresh change of underwear from a woman who made sure I got the right size. A pair of grey sweats would replace my stinky, long-unwashed jeans.

After getting outfitted, Naomi and I found Kimarie and Gideon. The man who had stayed with them even led us to the location where the free shuttle bus would take us to the motel. We were clearly too disoriented to figure it out on our own.

The motel wasn't the Ritz, but the shower and nap were worth the hundred dollars we paid for our five hours' stay. In the morning, we left for the airport dressed rather oddly. Along with the grey sweatpants, I wore a button down dress shirt and brown loafers with white socks. I looked hilarious. Gideon was reduced to wearing his sister's remaining pink and white striped outfit.

In our last waiting room before boarding a flight from Philadelphia to Seattle, the children amiably made the rounds to greet every baby they could find. They made friends with grandfatherly folks. It was still a grand adventure in social exploration to them. The waiting area was crowded. When the gate attendants called for early boarding, they began with passengers with special needs and small children. We got into a short line circling the ticket podium. I was carrying Naomi and a backpack, and Kimarie was carrying Gideon and a backpack.

There were businessmen in pressed suits standing all around. Before we reached her, the lady with the microphone at the podium announced they were ready for elite traveler boarding, and the surrounding men began to press forward with their tickets outstretched in their hands. One poor unsuspecting guy moved to step right in front of us. "Excuse me!" I said with some force. Everyone within earshot noticed the tension and looked around. I focused a ferocious glare at him and mentally crushed his skull until he backed up and apologized. I partly felt bad for my outburst. How were people around us to know what we had been through? They were just trying to get to their meetings on a regular workday in America.

We boarded the last five-hour flight to Seattle. After rearranging seats with some other passengers whose groups were also split up, we sat in the very last row on the left. Naomi and Gideon had already taken whatever naps they figured they needed, and continually switched back and forth from Mommy's lap to Daddy's, or climbed the seats, or opened and closed the window shade.

Airlines had stopped serving meals since the last time we'd flown domestically. We were surprised to learn that instead they had snack boxes for sale. By the time a flight attendant reached us in the back row, the only snack box left was a combination of candy and chocolate cookies – the kind of stuff that we had already been eating for days. After learning our story, she felt horrible. With determination, she ventured forward on a quest to take care of us. She returned awhile later with a bag of bruised peaches donated by a kind woman in first class. We dipped into our own remaining stores and found a medium sized bag of pretzels, which we combined with the sticky fruit – an unsatisfying and messy meal.

A Lebanese-American woman sat directly in front of us with her children. They may have been the only others on the plane who had also been evacuated. Their wardrobe hadn't suffered as ours had. The woman might have been the wife of a diplomat. Perhaps she was married to a businessman and had gone home to Lebanon on vacation. She was obviously wealthy, judging from the size of the rock in her wedding ring. They had likely never been in any danger in Lebanon – none of the close calls we had experienced in the South. For them, the whole experience had been an adventure for her kids, who were excited to have ridden a

US Navy ship to Cyprus. After the announcement that we would be landing soon, she fussed with makeup and groomed her hair to prepare for our arrival.

We didn't have any bags to reclaim when we landed at SeaTac International Airport. As we ascended the escalator from the baggage claim area, a TV news film crew waited at the landing above. I mentally prayed the man with the microphone wouldn't notice our obvious castaway-style attire and attack us for an interview, but he was looking for someone else. The wealthy lady from our plane had checked a box on her evacuation form and arranged for the interview. She smiled for the camera and told about her suffering.

I viewed that woman disdainfully at the time. We'd endured so much more than she had. But on the spectrum of the history of exiles, our own experiences were nearly as cosmetic as hers.

We had resourceful families to rejoin. We had passports from our powerful government, which advocated for us, and sent trained military to rescue us. We spent *a day* in a transit camp, inconvenienced on our way back to normalcy. We had a credit card to order readily available food, when it wasn't simply offered to us. Yes, we acquired some perspective for compassion toward the true refugees in the world.

Our mothers were relieved to welcome us in the arrivals area. They'd also been tortured by the waiting. I nearly forgot that my mom had not yet met Gideon in person until she offered to hold him. She didn't seem to mind his girly costume.

After a real meal in a restaurant near the airport, we rode the final excruciating hours through rush hour traffic with Kimarie's mom to the Ware residence in Mount Vernon. The total elapsed time from the convent in Jounieh to the Ware's house was sixty-six hours. Kevin and Kari re-introduced our children to toys. Kimarie and I slept like we were dead.

Dear Family and Friends,

We arrived back at SeaTac airport shortly before noon. I am writing now after some desperately needed sleep and food.

As much as we love the idea of being surrounded by all of our loved ones, we anticipate needing a week or two to be able to fully function socially. Please be patient with us as we sort out the trauma, grief, and ongoing concern for dear friends who are still in mortal danger.

We are so thankful for all who prayed for us. Praise God for our rescue. He is so good.

Many of you have asked how you can assist us financially. Kimarie and I have to talk this over a little more to figure out how to answer. Initially, we *want* to say that there are others who need more help than we do, but then again we are going to have to start all over here. I will get back to you soon about ways that you can help us and with information on how to send relief to Lebanon as well.

We have heard secondhand reports from some of our friends in Tyre that conditions are worsening for them. A sister of one of the new believers was injured by flying shrapnel. There are few medical supplies remaining. They only have bread and hummus to eat.

In a little while we will touch base again. I am looking forward to answering all of your personal messages. It will be helpful in my own healing process.

Salaam,

Nate

DEBRIEFING

Two weeks later after my initial email describing the Hezbollah kidnapping, we were in another world. Not only had we survived, but we somehow achieved hero status. Newspaper reporters interviewed us. We received invitations to tell our story at gatherings.

After one presentation at my mom's church on Vashon Island, an old friend was eager to welcome us back. "I was on the edge of my seat, reading your emails," she said. "I checked my inbox every hour. It was so hard to tell what was best for you to do. Should you go? Should you stay? You were wise to drive to Beirut when you did. It was God's will. He brought you safely back to us."

Her thoughtfulness touched me. I said, "We're sure grateful to be here. Thanks so much for praying for us." I knew she sincerely cared for us, but I struggled to agree with her assessment.

Kimarie and I talked about it on the drive home. The memories of waiting and wondering what to do were still fresh and we needed to process what we'd been through. "Before we drove out of Tyre," I said, "every single person who gave us advice said it was wise to stay put and wait for the Marines. Do you remember feeling wise either way at the time?"

Kimarie laughed, "I don't think wisdom came into play much."

"Me neither. And would it have been any less God's will if one or all of us had been killed? I mean, we don't have guarantees that everything will turn out all right just because we follow him."

"Anything could have happened." Kimarie agreed. "Good people die every day. What makes us any different?"

Kimarie leaned over the seat to give Naomi and Gideon a snack. I sensed that whatever thoughts were about to come would be important to both of us in discerning the worth of our time in Lebanon and would impact future decisions.

Nothing had turned out the way we expected. Why did God call us to Lebanon to help people adore Jesus, and then allow this war to scatter us all, just when things were starting to go well? Even as I tried to reason through my emotions, I found my hard questions didn't dampen my faith. God was still good. He was still working out his best plan for our lives. What gave me peace of mind was knowing we had obeyed what we felt God wanted us to do. When Jesus said, "Follow me," we did.

Kimarie settled back into her seat. The kids were munching away happily. I shared my thoughts. "No matter what happens in our lives, I think if I know we're actively listening to God and responding to him, our lives will be satisfying."

Kimarie nodded and tried out the idea for herself. "Satisfaction," she said, "comes from knowing we've simply obeyed."

Simply obeying is different from obeying simply. It's not just about achieving the minimum requirements. I recall a preacher on a long ago Sunday morning. He asked us to imagine a big circle, like a fence. He said, "We constantly have the opportunity to retreat deeper into the center of the circle where Jesus is, but we prefer to hang out on the edges, the periphery of what is allowed. We push the boundaries. We want to hang out with those who are jumping the fence or taunting us from the lawless territory outside the circle."

He wanted us to embrace the goodness of God's biblical direction. I believed what the guy said. God knows what is best for us and is faithful to guide those who submit to him – a good message. But something wasn't quite right with the analogy. Why did it bother me?

Then it hit me. It had to do with the circle. It sounded too much like a cage. The illustration needed to be turned inside-out. A fence exists, but Jesus roams freely on the outside. The enclosure instead surrounds a finite number of prohibited activities about which God says, "Thou shalt not."

Following Jesus is getting *out* of jail, but people still congregate around the boundaries. Those who obey *simply* prefer to stand on the bottom boards of the fence looking back into the corral because it's familiar – comfortable. The idea of turning our backs on the forbidden zone and walking away is scary. Uncharted territory lies ahead across fields of freedom. We're exhausted at the mere suggestion of trying to keep up with Jesus, who's always on the move. It turns out God doesn't want simple obedience after all, if we take simple to mean minimalistic. He designed people to find satisfaction in obeying *radically*.

I pulled the car to the side of the road and parked in line for the next ferry to leave Vashon. I killed the engine and stepped down on the car's parking brake. For most of my life, the twenty-minute wait would have annoyed me. Instead, I smiled for the feeling of restful safety, compared to waiting in line to cross the Litani River.

How easy it would be to slip into a comfortable rhythm. Maybe I'd go back to work at the grocery store and come home from my eight-hour sentence to a warm TV and an entertaining meal. We'd done our part, right? We'd sacrificed enough. Now we deserved a break.

The temptation to trade away a satisfying life of following Jesus for sedated irrelevance scared me more than guided missiles. Our seven-year absence from the States enabled us to see our own culture with fresh objective eyes. Every day our Western culture bombards us with subtle gratuitous alternatives to choosing obedience.

In Tyre, Denis, Edmond, and their families were more than good friends. We practically treated each other's homes as our own. We depended on each other in that place where few followed Jesus. Now, more than ever Kimarie and I needed a circle of like-minded brothers and sisters around us, to keep us on track – to mutually challenge each other on to greater exploration outside the fence. Would we find a new community of friends in the land of independence? We weren't so sure.

The ferry arrived, and we boarded with the other cars. The kids begged to go upstairs to the passenger deck, which reminded me of how much my dad had hated my brothers and me running around the ferry when I was a kid. We went up and stood over the railing in the aft of the boat and watched the island slip away in the distance, surrounded by the salt water of Puget Sound like a castle's moat.

Driving off the ferry that day and onto the open road, we began a new and dangerous chapter to our lives, rediscovering our own identities at home with no boundaries.

EPILOGUE

For a while after we returned to the Seattle area, we were concerned for Naomi. "The Jet City" had lots of jets, and whenever one flew overhead she would fearfully look up at us and ask, "Boom, boom?" It didn't take long for her to recover. Kids are resilient.

Denis returned to Lebanon just a couple weeks after the war ended in August. He had many opportunities to lead in relief efforts. One particular project restored clean water for an entire village through the installation of a massive pump.

Though he was busy, Denis offered to go to our flat and retrieve some of the stuff we would come and get later. He went, but when he tried the key, he found that it no longer fit the lock. A note bearing a phone number was taped to the door, and its message read:

"Call us. We are very sorry and thank you. –Hezbollah."

We learned that Hezbollah had prepared for a complete Israeli invasion by controlling all the apartments vacated when the regular population fled. They changed the locks so that fighters could alternate locations to evade detection. Our home had apparently hosted some of these guys.

Denis called the number but was informed that he would only be allowed inside if the key master heard first from my own mouth that Denis should be let in. It felt surreal to me as I called from my in-laws' home and prepared myself to speak Arabic once again. I was about to thank Hezbollah for carefully guarding my belongings and give them permission to release the keys to my friend. When Denis later gained access to the apartment the only evidence he found of Hezbollah's stay in our place was a teapot-shaped burn mark on the kitchen carpet.

Life in Lebanon eventually returned to normal. Denis resumed English classes at the language center. The community of believers was expanded and refined.

In the spring of 2007, nearly a year after our return to the US, Kimarie and I left the kids with her parents and went back to Lebanon to reclaim our belongings and seek closure. Denis picked us up at the airport and followed an unusual detour back to his house to avoid a stretch of freeway that hadn't been repaired yet. Reaching the first traffic circle in Abbassieh on the outskirts of Tyre, and then passing the hospital where Naomi and Gideon were born, we felt the familiar sensation of arriving home.

One of our first stops was dinner at Tyros for the garlic saturated fatayl that we missed so much. How many birthday parties had we celebrated there? I had made my dabke dancing debut with Mustafa and twenty others on that dance floor. More recently, Naomi had toddled around, visiting all of the tables, welcomed by broad smiles from the other diners.

We climbed the eleven flights of stairs to our old apartment and were received warmly by our neighbors. We spent the afternoon together – heard their stories and retold ours. We sat on their balcony and shared the sunset over the Mediterranean one last time. Kamel and Amina retreated to the kitchen to make Arabic coffee. I stood and propped my elbows on the railing, leaning out to savor the view. I could see the obelisk in the center of the hippodrome casting its long shadow like a sundial measuring out the passage of time. The triumphal arch glowed reddish-orange as it had in countless sunsets past.

God has been active in Tyre throughout history – long before I arrived as a naive, single guy in 1999. He used this city of people to change me in ways that couldn't have happened anywhere else. Now God has written my family into Tyre's story, too. We are connected.

Someday, when I finish my race, I'd like my children to mingle my ashes with the ancient dust between the pillars of the aqueduct – next to the road where Jesus walked. Perhaps my last words to them will be, "Wait until spring and enjoy the orange blossoms.

"Carry on."

As for the other events of Nate's life in Lebanon, and all he did including photos and maps, are they not written in the annals of www.CoffeeAndOrangeBlossoms.com?

31081160R00121

Made in the USA
Charleston, SC
05 July 2014